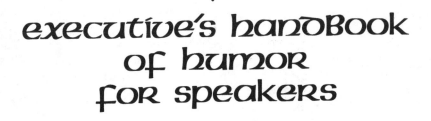

executive's handbook of humor for speakers

executive's handbook of humor for speakers

BUREAU OF BUSINESS PRACTICE
Waterford, Connecticut 06386

Printed in the United States of America

ISBN 0-87622-022-7

Reprinted 1985
Fifth printing

PREFACE

"If you've got something funny to do, you don't have to be funny doing it."

That's always been one of Charlie Chaplin's basic principles, and it goes a long way toward explaining his success.

Here's an example:

There's a sequence in *City Lights* where he's about to take part in a boxing match. He's sitting on a rubdown table in the dressing room, wearing his trunks, gloves, and derby, and his opponent comes in. Chaplin is seeing him for the first time, and he's a powerful brute of a guy, cold-eyed and ominous.

The sight of him makes Chaplin so nervous that he has to go to the bathroom to relieve himself. But as he reaches the bathroom door, he suddenly realizes he's wearing boxing gloves.

So he turns right around and climbs back on the rubbing table.

That's all. No double-take. No funny faces. He doesn't even permit himself that famous helpless shrug.

He simply climbs back onto the rubbing table and sits there.

But the scene is incredibly, hilariously, funny. It "slaughters" audiences. Strong men by the thousands have grabbed for their sides and howled themselves helpless over it.

What's funny about it? The material itself. Had Chaplin tried to *be* funny while playing the scene, he would only have weakened it. In other words, he had such a wonderful "bit" there, all he had to do was let it play itself.

"If you've got something funny to do, you don't have to be funny doing it."

Way Out There in Left Field

The Chaplin principle applies to using humor in

speeches. In fact, the "Chaplin" is the single basic requirement for using humor in speeches *effectively*!

Think it over.

The executive who's asked to make a speech is asked to for only one reason—he's got something to say that his audience will be interested in. Something about business, education, agriculture, aviation, labor relations, or whatever it is he's qualified to talk about. His audience hasn't filled the hall to hear him make jokes or do imitations.

They're there only because he's got something to say that will somehow inform, educate, or enlighten them. And it's essential that his entire presentation be directed to that end. If not, he'll lose them.

If he gets too far away from his subject, some members will drift out there into left field with him, but they won't bother to come back. And if he gets too far away from an appropriate tone, the same thing will happen. Which is to say that if the speaker gets too far away from the essential seriousness of his subject—if he gets too deep into funny stories and the pyrotechnics of "stand-up" humor—he'll find himself in trouble.

When he's ready to be serious, his audience probably won't be. They'll be too caught up in his being funny. They won't be able to make the switch.

So the speaker on serious themes, who's going to use humor to help him pace, lighten, and highlight his talk, has got to take that as another fundamental—he's got to be sure his humor never overwhelms his subject.

Humor is an adjunct—an aid. It's Worcestershire sauce and good, sharp mustard.

It's never the meat and potatoes!

Groucho Marx would be a poor choice to address a businessmen's convention concerned with the pros and cons of the high protective tarriffs. So would Bob Hope, Buddy Hackett, Flip Wilson, and Bill Cosby.

They're all too funny. They're all funny-men. They'd "paralyze" the audience with their gags, cracks, routines.

But what kind of a contribution would they make to the subject of their talk—"The Pros and Cons of the High Protective Tariff Insofar as It Affects American Business"? How could anyone concentrate on their serious material after laughing himself into a case of aching ribs over their routines?

What's funny? What's serious? You can't expect an audience to swing back and forth from one to the other over too wide a range.

Don't Need a Funny-Man Style

Proceeding from this last point:

To use humor in speeches effectively is to *insert* it, *insinuate* it, *work it into the subject matter of the speech*—not stick it out there where it stands apart! But this approach (deft, subtle, and finely tuned to your audience's mood and make-up) puts the emphasis on *content*, not *style*.

In short, *you* don't have to be funny. You don't have to be a *funny-man*! But you do have to have funny *material*.

If you're going to tell a joke or story, it's got to be a joke or story the audience you're telling it to will find funny. It doesn't make any difference whether or not your wife thinks it's funny. It doesn't really make any difference whether or not *you* think it's funny. The only thing that matters is whether or not your audience thinks it's funny.

If they don't (which is to say if you've selected poor material), you're probably going to find yourself trying to *make* it funny by the way you tell it. That means funny faces, accents, imitations, or whatever—the devices and techniques of the professional funny-man.

And as you do that, your humor will inevitably separate itself from your subject, separate itself from whatever it is you've been asked to talk about. Instead of being integrated, worked into your speech, it's become a thing in itself.

It's not strengthening your speech, adding to its effectiveness. It's detracting from it.

Once your audience is involved with you as a comic, a funny-man (even a good one, incidentally), you're no longer able to do the job you've been asked to do. *You're no longer able to involve them with you as a serious-minded man with something important to say.*

They won't buy it!

So the funny presentation, the funny-man style, defeats its purpose. It distracts your audience, distorts its mood, gets it thinking of you as an entertainer.

And that's all wrong! You shouldn't let it happen.

What's needed then is simply this: the right joke or story, which means the right joke or story for that particular audience.

Tell it straight. Tell it cheerful. Tell it as though you think it's funny. Let them see you enjoy it. That's all you need.

Anything more than that is excessive.

Which gets us back to Chaplin's principle.

"If you've got something funny to do, you don't have to be funny doing it."

What's Funny to Some . . .

Okay—what's funny? What's funny *material*? Never mind Red Skelton getting a laugh by letting his pants fall down. What's funny *material*?

Well, what's funny to businessmen isn't necessarily funny to farmers. And what's funny to teachers isn't necessarily funny to automobile salesmen.

So in a certain sense, everything's funny and nothing's funny. It all depends on who's considering it. The point is obvious. *To a very great degree, successful humor* (particularly as used in a speechmaking context) *is category humor.*

There are *categories* of funny jokes and stories, and *categories* of audiences. The trick is to mesh them most effectively. The right material for the right audience.

The teachers' joke for the teachers' convention. Maybe the *literary* joke for the teachers' convention—it's a possibility. It's a better possibility if they're English teachers than if they're mathematics teachers.

With mathematics teachers, maybe a joke involving the use of an abacus would work better— it's a possibility.

And so forth. It's a question of logical connections, sound meshing. It's a question of making the right selections from a large assortment of jokes, stories and other forms of verbal humor.

INTRODUCTION

The *Executive's Speech Course* is based on this principle: Humor is essential to an effective speech. It has a place in making a speech lively, giving it a change of pace, emphasizing key points. There are right and wrong ways to use humor.

Then there is the matter of the actual art of speaking. There are techniques of delivery that you can and should study; they will improve the way you deliver your speech. A special section in the *Executive's Speech Course* is devoted to this.

USE THIS UNIQUE INDEX

1. All jokes are listed alphabetically by subject for quick, effective use.

2. All jokes are numbered and cross-referenced to give you a wealth of stories on any subject, thus allowing you to choose the most appropriate one for your speech.

3. The *Story Index* can be used as a great idea starter.

NOW LOOK THROUGH THE STORY FILE AND STORY INDEX, AND THEN READ THESE SIMPLE INSTRUCTIONS.

In addition to the categories from the *Story File*, you'll find other headings which are related to those in the *File* plus a cross-referencing system. Thus, if you can't find what you want right away in the *Story File*, turn to the *Story Index*. You'll almost certainly find the joke you need.

HOW TO FIND THE APPROPRIATE JOKE

Step 1: If you have a topic in mind, look it up in the *Story File* just as you would locate a word in the dictionary.

Step 2: Then turn to the *Story Index* and look under the same topic. The numbers following each category will refer you to other jokes in other categories which are related to the topic you have in mind.

NUMBERING

The number of each joke appears directly above it and is not related to the page number. The numerals before the decimal point relate it to other jokes in the same category (all the jokes on "Marriage" begin with 494), while the numerals after the decimal point differentiate it from the others within that category (e.g., 494.01, 494.02, etc.).

Example: Suppose you were interested in finding jokes on the subject of politics. Turn to the "P-T" section of the *Story File;* there you will find jokes dealing with some aspect of "Politics/Politicians." For more on the same subject go to the *Story Index* and look up the numbered jokes listed after "see also." Locate these jokes numerically and you'll find that they also deal with "Politics/Politicians" even though they are classified under different headings.

ABILITY

2.50

Poise—The ability to keep talking while somebody else picks up the check.

2.51

Horse sense: The intuitive ability that keeps horses from betting on people.

2.52

Tact is the ability to make a person see the lightning without letting him feel the bolt.

2.53

A bandaged applicant for a divorce told the judge: "The woman just isn't safe to live with. She has been throwing things at me ever since we've been married."

The judge asked, "So why are you coming in after 19 years?"

The man responded, "Because her aim is getting better."

2.54

Behind every successful man is a surprised wife.

2.55

The Florida real estate firm's brand-new salesman asked the boss if he should refund the money to a burned-up customer who complained that the lot he bought was under water.

"What kind of salesman are you?" demanded the boss. "Sell him a boat!"

2.56

"Who do you think you are—a fireman or something?" asked the highway patrolman of the driver of a car he had just stopped. "The speed limit here is 50 miles an hour, and you were doing 85!"

"No, sir, I'm not a fireman. I'm a salesman, and a good one, too. I'll bet I can even talk you out of giving me a ticket."

"I'm afraid you'll lose this sale, buddy," said the patrolman. "Doing 85 in a 50-miles zone is no joke."

"But I wasn't driving 85, or 75, or even 50. As a matter of fact, I wasn't even going 10 miles an hour," said the salesman. He then proceeded with a long, involved explanation citing the theory of relativity plus a goodly number of fictional facts he made up on the spot.

But it was to no avail. Though he convinced the patrolman of the fact that he had, indeed, not been speeding he nevertheless got a ticket for illegal parking!

2.57

"Here is a typewriter that will do half your work for you."

"Great, give me two of them."

2.58

The office boy approached his boss one day and asked, "Would it be O.K. with you, Mr. Jones, if I used the company station wagon on the second Saturday of next month?"

"It's highly irregular to use company vehicles for personal business," replied the boss. "However, if it is in the nature of an emergency, we might be able to make an exception. Why do you want to use the car?"

"Well, Mr. Jones, that's the day I'm getting married."

"Wonderful," said the boss enthusiastically. "And who is the lucky girl?"

"I'm not sure yet. I didn't want to ask anyone until I could be sure I could get the car."

ACCIDENTS

10.50

Traffic cop: "Sir, your wife fell out of your car about two blocks back."

Husband: "Thank God. I thought I'd gone stone deaf."

10.51

The reason there were fewer accidents in the horse and buggy days is that drivers didn't have to rely completely on their own intelligence.

10.52

Judge: "You say it was an accident that you shot your wife?"

Man: "Certainly was. She stepped in front of my mother-in-law just as I pulled the trigger."

10.53

Out on a lonely highway one night, a speeding car crashed through a guard rail, leapt over a retaining wall, rolled down an embankment, and came to rest on its back in a creek.

A state policeman, arriving on the scene almost immediately, said, "What's the matter—are you drunk or something?"

"Of course, I'm drunk," said the driver. "What do you think I am—a stunt driver?"

10.54

I'll never forget the day I crashed into a police car and woke up two cops!

10.55

A young sailor was in a hurry to get home for the week-end. He wasn't quite sure how the accident happened or who was to blame, but he knew there had been a tremendous collision and much property damage. The other driver, observing the wreckage, said, "Well, it's lucky that neither of us was hurt badly. Let's go get a drink and settle our nerves until the cops come."

The seaman concurred, and the two stepped into a near-by pub. Still very nervous, the swabbie quickly downed a double. When he noticed that the other glass was still on the bar, he asked, "Aren't you going to drink yours?"

"No," said the other man, "I think I'll wait until after the police check around."

10.56

The old-timer who was suing over an automobile accident was on the stand and the defense counsel took over.

"Did you or did you not," the lawyer demanded, "at the time of the accident, when asked if you were injured, say that you were not?"

The old fellow answered: "It was like this. I was just heading down the road in my wagon, and along comes this one and knocks me and the horse into the ditch. He stops his car, looks at us, and sees that my horse has a broken leg. So he goes to his car, gets a gun, and shoots him. Then he says to me, 'Are you hurt?'"

10.57

The tycoon's neighbors were still talking about the night he arrived home after a late-evening convention. "I saw it all," said one. "Can you imagine? He roared into his driveway, clipped a tree, tore up 20 feet of hedge, knocked over the yard light and smashed into his garage door."

"It must have been terrible," replied another neighbor. "But it would have been worse. Can you imagine the damage he could have done if he'd been driving a car?"

10.58
Woman showing well-dented car to garageman: "The fender's been acting up again."

10.59
The crack salesman was given a rare old bottle of Kentucky sippin' whiskey as a gift at the office Christmas party. On his way home, he tripped over a sled that had been left on the sidewalk. He tumbled tail over teakettle, smacked against a patch of ice, and ended up sprawled against a tree. Suddenly he felt something warm trickling down his leg.
"God," he moaned, "I hope that's blood."

10.60
"What happened?" asked the woman.
"Nothing much," said the conductor. "We hit a cow."
"Was it right there on the tracks?"
"No, lady, we chased it over the meadow and through the woods to the barn!"

10.61
A man was applying for a job as a switchman for the railroad.
"Tell me," said the station manager, "what would you do if you saw two trains coming at each other on the same track?"
"I'd switch one of them right off and onto another track."
"And what if the lever was stuck?"
"I'd run right out with a red flag and wave one of them down."
"And what if the engineer didn't see you?"
"I'd call my mother."
"Call your mother! What could she do?"
"Nothing, but she loves to see train wrecks."

10.62

Examining the garage bill from his wife's latest mishap, a moaning husband asked, "Wasn't $25 quite high to tow the car to the garage?"

"Yes, I thought so. But don't you worry, I got your money's worth. I kept the brakes on while they towed me in."

10.63

A driver was picked up unconscious after an accident and was being carried to a nearby filling station. Suddenly he opened his eyes and began to struggle frantically to get away. He later explained that, when he opened his eyes, someone was standing in front of the "S" in the "Shell" sign.

10.64

A rather stout woman consulted her attorney about suing over an accident in which she had lost a thumb.

"But," asked the lawyer, "what makes you think your thumb is worth $50,000?"

"Because," said the woman firmly, "it was the one I kept my husband under."

10.65

A woman was driving along the highway and flicked on her left rear signal light. A cabbie behind her saw the blinking light and pulled over to the right lane to pass. But then the lady suddenly turned right, directly in front of him. The obvious happened. The lady, unhurt, but furious, leapt out of her battered car, ran over to the shaken cabbie and screamed: "Didn't you see my signal?"

"I sure did, lady," he said, "but it was blinking left."

"Of course it was," she shouted, "I was signaling you to go left."

10.66

Wife to husband: "I put a little scratch on the bumper, dear. If you want to look at it, it's in the back seat."

10.67

A slightly inebriated motorist was driving too fast, lost control, and smashed into a telephone pole. When he came to, he was on the ground grasping an armful of telephone wires. "Thank God," he mumbled, "it's a harp."

10.68

"Where did you get the black eye?"

"In a railway accident."

"But I didn't hear about a train wreck."

"I didn't say there was a train wreck. I was on a train going through a tunnel and kissed the father instead of the daughter."

10.69

"My baby just swallowed a .45 caliber bullet!" shouted the distraught mother as she raced into the drug store. "What shall I do?"

"Give him a good strong laxative," answered the pharmacist, "but, for Pete's sake, don't point him at anyone!"

ADVERTISING

20.50

The sports editor was interviewing a college coach. "What's your line-up for next season?" he asked.

"Well, I can't be sure at this point," was the reply, "but as of now it looks like this: Jackson, Lendowski and Watson will do the razor blade commercials; Hirsh, Smith and Taylor will go to deodorants; Russell and Stern will appear for shaving cream; and Samson is slated for breakfast cereals."

20.51

The wife of a New York ad man was putting their seven-year-old son to bed and said, "George, say your prayers."

He began: "Dear God. Please bless Mom and Dad and give us this day our oven-baked, slow-rising, vitamin-enriched bread."

20.52

Writing ads is a vicious circle. So says my copywriter friend. He writes an ad. They pay him. They print the ad. His wife reads it. Then he pays for it.

20.53

The rookie quarterback was a phenomenal success. His abilities on the field were unequaled in the history of the game. After a particularly impressive victory, a sportswriter asked the athlete, "Just what is it you attribute your success to?"

"Well, I really can't explain it," said the gridiron great. "Right now, I'm negotiating with two different cereal companies."

20.54

The advertising business is filled with young men in high positions. There's one story about a young fellow who joined an agency as a trainee on Monday at a salary of 75 bucks a week and was such a hotshot advertising man that by Friday he had been made a vice president. The chairman of the board called him in and congratulated him on his magnificent success with the company and informed him he would be the guest of honor that night at an executive dinner. "Thank you, sir," said the youngster, "I'm so pleased I just can't wait to tell Mommy!"

20.55

The advertising man wanted to make sure his direct mail letters got into the hands of every married woman in the area. So he addressed the envelopes to the husbands and marked them "Personal."

20.56

The sign outside the church read: IF TIRED OF SIN, COME IN. And beneath it, scrawled in lipstick, was the message: "If not, call Gladys at 737-9231."

20.57

When a prominent clergyman was asked to comment about the state of advertising in America, he declined. But he did allow that he would pray fervently for those who made their living at it.

20.58

Classified ad in a New England newspaper: "For sale: handsome secondhand tombstone. Outstanding bargain for a family named Perkins."

20.59

There was a big blast going on in a California town when an earthquake hit. The host of the big party tried to keep his head as homes fell and water mains burst. He rushed his guests outside, and then raced back into the house to see if he'd missed anybody.

He found one man still in the bathroom, with water up to his waist. The man muttered, "Honest, Herb! All I did was pull the handle!"

20.60

"What every young girl should know before she weds," promised the ad. "Profusely illustrated. Explicit instructions. Sent in a plain wrapper." Every eager buyer who clipped the coupon received a cookbook.

20.61

It is said that Samson had the right idea about advertising. He took two columns and brought down the house.

20.62

You can really tell autumn is in the air. The shaving cream commercials are being done by football players.

ADVICE

22.50

The two stenos met at the drinking fountain. "I don't know what I'm going to do," said one. "My boy friend's birthday is coming up and I don't know what to get him. What do you give a man who has everything?"

The other steno looked up with a shy smile and replied: "Encouragement, dear, encouragement."

22.51

Two bums in New York's Bowery were commiserating over the common roots of their fate. "I'm a fellow who never listened to anybody."

"Shake, partner, I'm a man who followed everybody's advice."

22.52

If you go through life with a clenched fist, nobody can ever put anything in it.

22.53

All my life, people have told me it is better to give than to receive. But you know, when I think about it . . . receiving isn't so bad!

22.54

A tourist stopped an old New Yorker and inquired, "Excuse me, sir, but can you tell me how to get to Carnegie Hall?"

To which the old-timer replied, "Practice, my boy, practice."

22.55

At the luncheon table, the tycoon was telling his friend about the many worries plaguing him. "They're closing in from all sides," he declared.

The sympathetic friend offered this advice: "I had the same problem, but I found a solution. Just lump together all the related problems, and you'll find you have less to worry about. It worked for me. I took all my problems, lumped them together, and I now have only three—nagging creditors, a profitless business, and the fact that I'm broke."

22.56

A robber baron businessman once told Mark Twain: "Before I die I mean to make a pilgrimage to the holy land. I will climb to the top of Mount Sinai and read the Ten Commandments."

To which Twain replied, "I have a better idea. Why don't you stay right at home and keep them."

22.57

If you must start something, be sure you can stop, too.

22.58

The man told me, cheer up, things could be worse. So I cheered up, and sure enough, things got worse.

22.59

We might be more eager to accept good advice if it did not continually interfere with our plans.

22.60

If the going seems easy, you're going downhill.

22.61

A few choice olives at the top of the jar is the best way to sell the small ones.

22.62

A wife sought the advice of a fortune teller, who prophesied, "Prepare yourself for widowhood! Your husband is about to die a violent death."

The wife sighed deeply and asked, "Will I be acquitted?"

22.63

When wine, women, and song become too much for you, stop singing.

22.64

Kibitzer: A guy who can always tell you what he'd do in your place, but who has no place of his own.

22.65

Good advice for a young girl: Marry a man with a strong will—made out to you!

22.66

Always put off till tomorrow what you are going to make a mess of today.

22.67

Applause is somewhat like the fountain of youth—enjoy the drink, but don't ever quite believe it.

AGE

30.40

"You should be ashamed of yourself," said dad to his lazy son. "When Abe LIncoln was your age he chopped wood for a living."

"Sure," said son, "and when he was your age he was President."

30.41

A famed stockbroker lay on his deathbed. A friend stopped by to visit, and said, "Come on, Harry. You'll be around to see 90."

Harry answered, "If the Good Lord can get me at 75, why should he wait until I go up to 90?"

30.42

My uncle's ninety-five and still chasing girls ... but he can't remember why.

30.43

This gal was so old that she was rock and roll queen of the War of 1812.

30.44

The train conductor looked down at the little lad and asked his mother how old he was.

"He's only four," she replied.

"And Mother," volunteered the boy, "is just thirty-five."

30.45

The average American woman is not old at forty, in fact she isn't even forty.

30.46

"Getting married?" said the doctor to the octogenarian. "How old are you?"

"Eighty-one," the man replied.

"And how old is the bride?" the doctor asked.

"Twenty-one," came the reply.

"But that much difference in age could mean death," the doctor warned.

The old man answered slowly, "Well, if she dies, she dies."

30.47

Finding a woman's true age is like looking at a used car. You look for a "telltale" to see if they've tried to turn the speedometer back.

30.48

Salesclerk: "What can I do about women customers who insist on talking about the low prices of the good old days?"

Manager: "Just act surprised and tell them you didn't think they were old enough to remember back that far."

30.49

One old gent said, "At my age, when a girl flirts with me in the movies, she is after my popcorn."

30.50

Youthful figure—Something you get when you ask a woman her age.

30.51

You can tell when you hit middle age by the way it hits back.

30.52

> Make your wife happy;
> It's easily done:
> Remember her birthday
> But forget which one.

30.53

Old age is when you get that morning-after feeling—without the night before!

30.54

A coed brought her roommate, a vivacious blonde, home for a weekend to meet her family, which included her great-grandfather. Making the introduction, the girl said, "And just think, Eloise, he's in his nineties."

"My early nineties," said the old fellow, with a half-forgotten gleam in his eye.

30.55

An elderly Broadway star went to a psychiatrist and complained about her husband's impotency. "How old are you?" asked the doctor.

"It's none of your business," she said, "but if you must know, I'm 84."

"And how old is your husband?"

"He's 93."

"And when did you first notice his disinterest in you physically?"

"Well," she said, "the first time was last night and again this morning."

30.56

An energetic old bachelor cuddled up to a sweet young thing in a bar and said, "Where have you been all my life?"

She said, "Well, for the first 30 years of it I wasn't even born."

30.57

When Old Man Gardner reached the ripe old age of 105, the local newspaper sent a reporter to interview him.

"To what do you attribute your long life?" asked the newsman.

"The real reason is that I have never touched a drop of liquor."

Just then there was an awful crash in the next room.

"What's that?" said the startled reporter.

"It's only my father," answered Gardner. "He always breaks things when he's drunk!"

30.58

A doctor asked a female patient her age.

"I never disclose my age," said the woman, "but as a matter of fact I have just reached twenty-five."

"Really?" said the doctor, "what detained you?"

30.59

At 20 a man thinks he can save the world. At 40 he's lucky if he can save part of his salary.

30.60

The old, gray-haired, former pioneer was being interviewed on his ninetieth birthday.

"Why do you think you've lived for 90 years?"

The old man shot back, "Primarily because I was born in 1881."

30.61

"You say that fellow's ninety-six years old and has never looked at a girl in his life, and doesn't drink, smoke, or gamble?"

"Yep, that's right. What gets me is why he wanted to live so long."

30.62

An old mountaineer was sitting in his favorite cane-backed rocker on the porch of his cabin, slowly rocking north and south. Nearby sat his forty-three-year-old son, rocking east and west. "Son," drawled the old man, "it's about time you learned not to wear yourself out that-away. Rock the way the board goes and save yer strength."

30.63

My whole problem started when I was only nine months old . . . I hated myself because I was too short.

30.64

Ideas are like beards: Men do not have them until they grow up.

30.65

"Did old Uncle Herbie die?"
   "Hope so. They buried him last week."

30.66

Old-timer: One who remembers when eight-forty-five was the time the play started, not the price of the ticket.

ALCOHOL
DRINKING

40.20

I took my mother-in-law out for a drink yesterday, and four bar flies immediately signed the pledge!

40.21

A fellow a few sheets to the wind stumbled out of a bar and poured himself into a taxi. "Take me to Broadway and Forty-Ninth," he ordered.

"You're at Broadway and Forty-Ninth, now," the driver told him.

"Fine," he said, fishing for his wallet. "But next time, don't drive so fast!"

40.22

A boozer is a guy you don't like who drinks as much as you do.

40.23

A tiny, green grasshopper jumped onto a bar. The man behind the bar watched the insect jump from one spot to another and finally said: "You know we have a drink named after you, little fellow?"

"Really?" said the grasshopper. "You have a drink named Sylvester?"

40.24

A Scot was sitting in a bar with an Irishman, when he noticed another Irishman lying on the floor.

"Good Lord," said the Scot, "he's drunk."

"No, he's not," replied the upright Irishman, "he moved."

40.25

A traveling salesman stopped in the Tennessee hills and asked an old mountaineer if he could spend the night. The old gent agreed, and they sat down on the porch. Then the mountain man produced a jug, and offered the stranger a drink.

"No thanks," came the reply, "I'm not a drinking man."

The oldster said, "I get offended when a man won't drink with me," and with that grabbed his double-barreled shotgun, pointed it at the salesman and said: "Drink!"

"Please," begged the younger man, "I don't want to hurt your feelings or be unneighborly, but I don't drink at all, not with anybody."

"Drink or I'll blow you off this mountain," screamed the old man. The salesman raised the earthenware jug to his lips and partook. He took several swallows, and then his face grimaced in pain.

"I don't care what you do to me, but this stuff is terrible," he barely whispered.

"I know," said the other, "now you hold the gun on me."

40.26

"What do you call a person who can put you in contact with the world of spirits?"

"A bartender."

40.27

I just had a great new idea for gardening . . . ya water your garden with whiskey, and raise stewed tomatoes.

40.28

A gent stepped up to a bar and asked for a martini compounded of 24 parts gin, one part vermouth. The bartender, startled but game, said, "Yes, sir. Like a twist of lemon?"

The gent grumbled, "If I want lemonade I'll ask for it."

40.29

The news raced down the street in old Dodge City. Black Pete was a-comin' into town.

Ned, the saloonkeeper, heard the news and was just about to close up shop when a huge man with a sinister black moustache walked in. He had a polecat in one hand and six rattlesnakes in the other. A massive buffalo rifle was slung over his shoulder and two six-guns sat holstered at his hip. "Gimme a whiskey or I'll tear your head off and shoot your heart out from the top!" he shouted.

Ned started pouring a shot, but the stranger grabbed the bottle and downed it in one gulp. "Do you want another?" Ned humbly mumbled.

"Yeah," said the man, "but make it fast. Black Pete is coming."

40.30

Tour guide in Dublin: "We are now passing St. James Gate brewery, the largest brewery in Ireland."
Tourist: "Why?"

40.31

A drunk appeared before the judge who said: "This is intolerable. You have been coming before me for 20 years."

To which the drunk replied, "Can I help it if you never get promoted?"

40.32

Pink elephant—A beast of bourbon.

40.33

A man explained how he made such good Martinis. "I take some gin and put it on the table in the kitchen. Then I put a glass of vermouth out on the porch. I open the windows. When the wind blows through the house, I have a perfect Martini."

40.34

Sir Winston Churchill, who had a well-known appreciation for an occasional drink, was scheduled to speak before a small gathering.

The chairman introduced him by saying, "If all the spirits consumed by Sir Winston were poured into this room, it would reach up to here on the wall."

He drew a line with his fingers at about eye level.

Sir Winston rose. He glanced at the imaginary line on the wall, then at the ceiling, then made a mathematical calculation with his fingers. Then he sighed and said, "Ah, so much to be done, and so little time in which to do it."

40.35

I had one of those new Boy Scout cocktails ... two of them and a little old lady has to help you across the street.

40.36

Spring is here—when nature sends out her "Buds" in six-packs!

40.37

Good wine is the drink of gods. Scotch is the drink of gentlemen, champagne is the drink of ladies, beer is the drink of youth. The next morning they all drink black coffee.

40.38

The inimitable W. C. Fields had a habit of taking a bottle of highly potent liquid with him to the set when he was making pictures. When asked, he always said the container was filled with nothing but pineapple juice.

As a prank one day, someone on the set snatched the bottle, emptied it, and refilled it with pineapple juice.

Discovering the switch, W. C. Fields roared, "Who put the pineapple juice in my pineapple juice?"

40.39

An intrepid explorer set out singlehanded for the Amazon jungle in Brazil. Authorities equipped him with all the necessary gear, topped off with a miniature bottle of gin, another of vermouth, and a tiny mixer.

"What's this for?" asked the explorer. "You know I don't drink."

"That's in case you're hopelessly lost, without another human around for miles," was the answer. "Mix yourself a martini. Somebody's absolutely certain to pop up and tell you, 'Don't make it that way—make it this way'."

40.40

I've got to give up drinking ... I'm starting to see the handwriting on the floor.

40.41

A banker got slightly loaded at a party but was determined to maintain his dignity when the hostess showed him her newborn twins.

He said, "Ah, what a beautiful child."

40.42

My uncle is so full of corn liquor that they had to shuck him before they could bury him.

40.43

Two sweet old ladies were trying to smuggle tequila across the Mexican border, but they were stopped by the border patrol.

The officer pointed to a flask and said, "What's that?"

"It's holy water," said one of the matrons.

The guard took a taste and said, "Wait a minute, this is tequila."

One of the ladies spoke up quickly, "My, my, my, another miracle."

40.44

A beautiful young poetess raised a glass of wine and said, "When I partake of the grape, the music of a thousand muted violins whispers in my ear, and I'm transported into a magic land of green rivers, forests, and castles. On the other hand, beer makes me burp."

40.45

A drunk was sitting next to a distinguished looking couple in a bar when he cut loose with a resounding burp.

"How dare you belch before my wife!" the man demanded.

"My most humble pardon, sir," said the drunk. "I wasn't aware that it was madam's turn."

40.46

My brother-in-law came home drunk one time and walked into the closet and said, "Third floor, please."

40.47

Two moonshiners were talking shop one day and one said, "When I take my brew to town, I always drive 15 miles an hour."

"Afeared of the law?" asked the other.

"Nope. Gotta age the stuff."

40.48

Comedian Jackie Gleason and restaurateur Toots Shor once agreed to have a drinking contest. They agreed to meet at Toots' when he closed the watering spot the next afternoon at 3:00.

Gleason arrived a few minutes early and saw Shor knocking one back.

"What are you doing? We're not supposed to start until three," said the comedian.

Shor answered, "Just hitting a few fungos."

40.49

A man who was somewhat inebriated was picked up by police who suspected he might be the burglar for whom they were seaching.

"What are you doing out on the streets at four o'clock in the morning?" he was asked.

"Going to a lecture," he said.

"At 4 a.m.?" was the decisive snort. "You expect us to believe that?"

"You sure would," sighed the drunk, "if you knew my wife."

40.50

Hear about the guy in (your town) who committed suicide? . . . He ate a sponge . . . then drank five quarts of beer.

40.51

Three drunks had a game they played every night at a local bar. They would sit and drink for a good while, then one would get up and leave the room. Then the other two would try to guess who left.

40.52

Seeing a fully equipped St. Bernard one day, W. C. Fields remarked, "Ah, man's best friend. And a dog."

40.53

In the Mekong Delta area of Vietnam, a medical officer was testing the water supply of a small forward reconnaissance team.

"What precautions do you take against contamination?" he asked the young sergeant in charge.

"Well, sir, first we boil it."

"Excellent."

"Then we filter it."

"Perfect."

"Then," said the sergeant, "for safety's sake, we drink beer."

40.54

Big George had been drinking beer all afternoon, and had dropped into an extremely chic restaurant to get something to eat.

"Bring me an order of sardines," he bellowed at the waiter.

The waiter replied, with only a slight touch of sarcasm, "And would the gentleman like them served in the can?"

George said, "Well, no, but you'd better hurry."

40.55

A seller of rare orchids in New York was discovered to be intoxicated most of the working day. He quickly acquired the nickname "petrified florist."

40.56

"What do you take for insomnia?"

"I always take a few shots of whiskey."

"Does that make you sleep?"

"No, but it makes me feel so good I want to stay awake."

40.57

I'll never forget my dad's last words . . . "I don't see how they can make this liquor for only a dollar a gallon."

40.58

The captain of a ship once entered "Mate was drunk today" in the ship's log. When the mate slept it off, he was angry and embarrassed. He pleaded with the captain to strike the entry, saying that it was the first time it had happened, and that it would not happen again. But the captain refused and said, "We must always write the exact truth in the log."

The next week the mate kept the log, and the first day he entered, "Captain was sober today."

40.59

In an obscure booze emporium on New York's Third Avenue, two slightly whoozy gentlemen discovered not only that both were Yale graduates, but that they were members of the same class. After many tearful embraces and just before both passed out, they swore to meet at the same bar, come hell or high water, 10 years later.

The first of them actually kept the date. He entered the place sheepishly, not believing there was one chance in a million the other would remember. But there, propped up at the bar, was Yale Man Number Two.

"What do you know," marveled Number One. "I never thought you'd even be able to find this joint after 10 long years!"

Number Two turned a bleary eye on him and growled, "Who left?"

40.60

A man was arrested for feeding straight bourbon to his pet bird. He was charged with contributing to the delinquency of a myna.

40.61

Two drunks went to a wake, but took a wrong turn and knelt down in front of the grand piano. They offered a few silent prayers, and then left. Outside, one said to the other, "I didn't know your friend, but he certainly had beautiful teeth."

40.62

A man was leaving for a hunting trip, and his wife asked him how he was planning to handle the preparation of meals.

"No problem," he said. "In the morning, Fred will mix breakfast. Then Herb will shake lunch, and I'll open the six-pack for dinner."

40.63

Jackie Cannon, well-known Broadway and Hollywood publicist, tells of the time when he was responsible for keeping a famous Hollywood personality from hitting the bottle while in New York on a picture-promotion tour. He accompanied the star around town for all their appointments. And each time the actor would want to stop at a bar for a drink, Cannon would talk him out of it.

Finally, the thirsty actor asked if it would be all right to get some candy to take his mind off drink. The publicist, thinking it a good idea, allowed it. When they went into the candy store, the star spotted some liquor-filled candies in the showcase and said to the owner, "Give me a quart of the middles."

40.64

A drunk was barely able to keep himself upright by holding on to a Montreal lamppost. He kept muttering, "It can't be done; it can't be done."

Finally a man came by and said, "What can't be done?"

As he fell to the ground, the drunk pointed to a sign across the street. It read, "Drink Canada Dry."

40.65

A drunk fell off a 14-story building. A cop raced up and said, "What happened?"

The drunk replied, "I don't know. Just got here myself."

40.66

"And what makes you so certain the defendant was in a state of complete intoxication?" the lawyer demanded of the cop.

The cop replied, "Because I saw him put a penny in a parking meter on Ninth Street then look up at the clock on the church and shout, 'Beautiful! Great, I've lost 20 pounds."

40.67

A drunk was approaching a large hotel just as two children spun all three revolving doors simultaneously.

The man looked at it for a minute and said, "They'll never get it off the ground."

40.68

An old British naval captain was told he had a disease that was the result of too much water in the body.

"But I've never taken a drop of water in my life!" he exclaimed. Then he thought about it for a minute and reflected, "Must have been all that bloody ice."

40.69

Three conventioneers in New York celebrated a bit too much, and on the way back to their hotel they ended up in the Bronx Zoo. After they had been standing in front of the lion cage for a while, two of them started to leave.

The third said, "You boys can leave if you want, but I'm gonna stay for the movie."

40.70

Teetotaler—A weak man who constantly yields to the temptation of denying himself a drink.

40.71

Father has so much liquor in him that he has to wear an internal revenue stamp.

40.72

A man was shipwrecked and captured by cannibals. Each day one would take a dagger and puncture one of his veins, and some of the natives would drink his blood.

Finally one day he said to the chief, "Look, I don't care if you eat me, but I hate to get stuck for drinks all the time."

40.73

Groucho Marx: "What's for dessert?"
Waiter: "Stewed prunes."
Groucho: "Didn't know they drank."

40.74

The only trouble with drinking beer is that it makes you feel like a fuel truck—round, heavy, and full of gas!

40.75

Another drunk was brought before a judge who began, "My man, you have been brought here for drinking."

"Great, your honor, let's get started," was his response.

AMERICA
AMERICANS

50.50

Two ladies were watching the annual St. Patrick's Day Parade in New York when one noticed that no other than Dublin Mayor Bobby Briscoe was leading the march.

"See that fella," said Sadie. "He's the Mayor of Dublin, Ireland, and he's Jewish!"

"Wonderful," exclaimed her companion. "Something like that could only happen in America!"

50.51

The best place to find out what shape the country is in is at the beach.

50.52

Faith: The thing which enables us to enjoy our religion, form of government, and hot dogs.

50.53

When the colonists came to this country, the Indians ran it. There were no taxes, no national debt, no air pollution. The women did all the work. And the white man thought he could improve a system that that?

50.54

An acquaintance of mine was touring London, and said "hello" to a Briton in Hyde Park. The chap returned the greeting, and then said: "American, aren't you? I can tell by your accent."

"You've got a nerve saying that," said the visitor, "you're the one with the accent."

50.55

An American moved to Paris to attend classes at the Sorbonne. Every day on his way to school, however, he passed a bakery where the owner was beating his only employee with a loaf of bread. Then one day he walked by and saw the underling being beaten with a cake.

His curiosity hit new highs; he ran over and said to the owner, "Why are you doing this?"

The man replied, "Today is his birthday."

50.56

A visiting expert from the United States went to a small African country and asked one of the natives what the death rate was in the country.

The native replied, "Same as everywhere else—one per customer."

50.57

The cycle of American life. Young farm boy works day and night to live in the city. Newly arrived city man works day and night to live in the country.

50.58

Will Rogers once said that Calvin Coolidge "was the first American president to discover that what the American people want most is to be left alone."

50.59

A man was passing a fish store that had two tubs of lobsters side by side. One tub read "$2 apiece," and the other "$3." While he was watching, a lobster from the two dollar barrel climbed up the side, worked his way over the top, and plopped into the three dollar tub.

"Ah," sighed the man, "only in America."

50.60

So many products are being called back, sometimes I think we lead the world in mess production.

50.61

We Americans are a strange lot. We devote one day a year to mothers and a whole week to pickles!

50.62

When she was sixteen, she was chosen Miss America . . . of course, in those days, there were very few Americans.

50.63

Everybody is now endowed with life, liberty, and some $2,000 worth of national debt.

50.64

The average American is for the underdog, but only on condition that he has a chance to win.

ANIMALS

60.30

Two fleas were talking and one said, "You wanna walk or take a dog?"

60.31

Q: What do you get when you cross a shark with an African walking catfish?

A: I don't now, but it will certainly get a seat on the ferry.

60.32

Two goats were standing behind the back lot at Paramount Pictures chewing on reels of film.

"How is it?" asked one.

"Not bad," said the other, "but I liked the book better."

60.33

"How do porcupines make love?" said the girl to the zoologist.

"Carefully," was the reply, "very carefully."

60.34

At the Bronx Zoo a kangaroo suddenly leaped 12 feet over the bars of his topless cage and took off in the direction of Yonkers at 80 miles an hour. A keeper dashed up to a baffled lady who had been standing in front of the kangaroo's cage and demanded, "What on earth did you do to that kangaroo to make him run that way?"

"Nothing really," the lady declared. "I just tickled him a little."

"You'd better tickle me in the same place," suggested the keeper grimly. "I've got to catch him!"

60.35

"You've got to hire this bear," said the man to the circus manager. "It can sing, dance, tell stories, and play the mandolin."

"Then why do you have it on a leash?" The manager asked.

"Have to," the man said, "he owes me 20 bucks."

The same manager then asked the man how he taught the bear the play the mandolin.

The man answered, "He took lessons."

60.36

Two lions were hiding in the savanna early one morning when a man walked by.

One lion said: "That man is a successful banker. Let's get him."

But his companion said: "Don't be absurd. No one puts the bite on a banker before nine o'clock."

60.37

You don't set a fox to watching the chickens just because he has a lot of experience in the henhouse.

60.38

Of all dogs, a St. Bernard is my favorite. Of course, I like anybody that can hold his liquor.

60.39

The missionary was being chased by the lion and, when he could run no farther, dropped to his knees and began praying fervently. To his surprise, the lion came along beside him and also began praying.

"This is wonderful," said the missionary, "for a minute I feared for my life."

"Will you shut up?" roared the lion. "Can't you see I'm saying grace?"

60.40

As the preacher tore through a fiery sermon about the Ten Commandments, the poor sinner burst into tears.

"Well, anyway," he said as the sermon came to a blazing finish, "I have never in my life made a graven image!"

60.41

I had to change my dog's name from Rover to Harriet . . . that way she can have puppies.

60.42

A customer, amused at the sight of the barber's dog, commented that it was touching to see a dog who liked to watch him cut hair.

"Well, it ain't that so much," he replied. "Sometimes I snip off a bit of a customer's ear."

60.43

Two apes were reading Desmond Morris' *The Naked Ape*, which noted that apes and similar animals had an inexplicable love for automobiles. Suddenly a beautiful female ape swung by. The first one leered at her, but the second said, "She's all right, but wouldn't you really rather have a Buick?"

60.44

St. Bernard: An animal which is half dog and half saloon.

60.45

Two cats were watching a tennis match. One was bored nearly to tears, but the other was watching intently.

"You're really digging this," said the bored cat.

"It's not really that," said the other. "My cousin Freddy is in the racket."

60.46

A mamma mouse and her two little ones were walking out one day. Suddenly they spied a cat. "Watch this," said the mother.

She walked near the cat and screamed, "BOW WOW!"

The cat yelped and raced up into a nearby tree.

The mother turned to her children and said, "See how important it is to know a second language."

60.47

Taxidermist—A guy who really knows his stuff.

60.48

"I want a poodle of which I can be proud," said a lady to a pet store owner. "Does that one have the proper pedigree?"

"Lady," the fellow replied, "If he weren't in that box, he wouldn't be seen dead with either of us."

60.49

Camel—a horse that was formed by a committee.

60.50

The easiest way to positively identify a wild bird in the forest is to be with a group of people who also don't know too much about them.

60.51

A New Yorker was driving through a barren wilderness in West Texas when a fancy bird skittled past the car. "What kind of fowl do you call that?" he asked.

The driver answered proudly, "That's a bird of paradise."

"Hm-m-m," mused the New Yorker. "Kind of far from home, isn't he?"

60.52

A lordly lion strutted out one morning and grabbed a baboon.

"Who is the king of the jungle?" he demanded.

"You are, oh mighty lion," was the quick response.

He then approached a gnu and repeated the question. The answer was the same. Then he glared at an elephant and asked again.

The pachyderm said nothing, but picked up the lion in his trunk, swung him around in the air, smashed him against a tree, and then stomped on him for two hours.

Beaten to a pulp, the lion muttered, "Just because you don't know the answer, you don't have to get sore."

60.53

Little Kathy brought home a cute little mongrel female dog, but just couldn't talk her mother into keeping it. At her wits' end, she looked out the window and saw the dog being pursued by a pack of male dogs.

"Come look, Mommy. Our dog's a natural leader."

60.54

A glib young man told the ticket agent at the bus station: "I'm very sorry, but I'm afraid my dog has eaten my ticket."

"Then I suggest you buy him a second helping," the agent said.

60.55

A Texas chicken farmer was driving his truck down the road and, at the same time, leaning out the window and bashing the cargo section with a piece of timber. Finally a policeman stopped him and asked him what he was doing. He replied, "I've got 5 tons of chickens back there, and this truck has a capacity of one ton. I've got to keep 4 tons in the air all the time."

60.56

A man boasted to his neighbor, "I got a cute little cocker puppy for my wife this morning."

"Gosh," sighed the neighbor, "I wish I could make a trade like that."

60.57

Visitors to a zoo were amazed to find a cage which was entitled, "Peaceful Coexistence," and held a fox and four chickens. The zoo keeper explained that it was easy to maintain the arrangement; all they had to do was occasionally toss in a few more chickens.

60.58

Eskimo dogs are the fastest dogs in the world . . . probably because the trees are so far apart up there.

60.59

Here's today's household hint . . . to catch your dog make a noise like a ham bone.

60.60

"They had to put poor Rover away today."

"That's a shame. Was he mad?"

"He wasn't exactly jumping for joy."

60.61

After the Flood ended and Noah ordered all the animals to go forth and multiply, he noticed two snakes still hanging around the ark.

"Go forth and multiply," he ordered.

"But we can't," said one, "we're adders."

60.62

For Sale: Prize English Bull Dog . . . eats anything . . . very fond of children.

60.63

Here's an important message to all the rabbits in America . . . STOP!

60.64

Why did the elephant and the mouse get married? They had to.

APPEARANCE

70.50

A man seven feet tall applied for a job as a lifeguard.

"Can you swim?" he was asked.

"No," he said, "but I can sure wade."

70.51

Lord Chesterfield once noticed a lethargic couple dancing the minuet, and remarked, "They look like they were hired to do it and were doubtful of being paid."

70.52

Ed Wynn was once telling a friend about something frightening that happened to a mutual friend, and said, "He turned as white as your shirt." He then took a closer look at the shirt and added, "Whiter."

70.53

Appearances are deceiving. A 10 dollar bill looks the same as it did 10 years ago.

70.54

She's the kind of girl you can't whistle at . . . your tongue is hanging out.

70.55

I know a beautiful girl who came to Hollywood hoping to break into pictures . . . and did she ever become famous! Producers went crazy over her . . . All the famous screen lovers made love to her . . . but she still didn't get into pictures.

70.56

After being given a tour of a building destined to become an architectural white elephant, President Grant was told by his guide that the building was "fireproof."

"What a pity," Grant replied.

70.57

A long-haired, pro-football guard was having his hair trimmed, when his barber teased, "I bet if I cut your hair off nobody would recognize you."

"That's probably right," he replied. "But then, I don't think people would recognize you either."

70.58

"You say that most of her beauty is inherited?"

"Right. Her uncle died and left her a drug store."

70.59

Barber: See this guy coming in? He'll want a shave.

Apprentice: Great. Can I practice on him?

Barber: Well, I suppose so, but be careful and don't cut yourself.

70.60

Don't make fun of that long-haired girl. It may be somebody's brother.

70.61

A night club performer once said to a female heckler, "My sweet, beauty is only skin deep, and you are beginning to peel."

70.62

My wife (girl) got a new hairdo yesterday . . . it looks like the nest of a sloppy eagle.

ARMED SERVICES

80.50

"I suppose now that you're gettin' discharged, you'll just wait for me to die so you can come and spit on my grave."

"Not me, First Sergeant. I ain't never going to stand in line again!"

80.51

An Italian friend of mine from New York got drafted and sent to the alien environs of an army base in the deep South. Every day his mother sent him a can of her special tomato sauce. He really didn't know what to do with it, so finally he poured it over his grits.

80.52

General (after a post parade): "Captain, what's the idea of marching all the tall men in front of all the short ones?"
Captain: "It's the lieutenant's fault, sir. He used to run a fruit store."

80.53

During a live fire drill in basic training, the sergeant addressed a rather slow recruit.

"Jones, those bullets can penetrate 36 inches of packed sand or two feet of solid wood. So keep your head down."

80.54

A man went into his local draft board and started screaming, "Take me right now. I want to kill and maim and mangle and defoliate and napalm and ... "

"Stop," shouted the clerk, "you're crazy."

"Write that down," came the quick reply.

80.55

I joined the army for three reasons: I wanted to defend my wonderful country . . . I knew it would help me physically and morally . . . and they came and got me.

80.56

Isn't that a wonderful idea—a TV commercial about the army and they're going to use all the successful techniques. Like a top sergeant comes out and a voice asks: "If he cussed you once, will he cuss you again?"

80.57

Captain (extremely irate): "Not a man on this ship will be given liberty this weekend."
Voice from the rear: "Give me liberty or give me death."
Captain: "Who said that?"
Voice: "Patrick Henry."

80.58

A seaman basic refused to jump off a 15-foot tower. The old chief upbraided him, saying, "What would you do if you were that high on a ship that was sinking?"

The lad replied, "Chief, I'd wait for it to sink another 10 feet or so!"

80.59

A second lieutenant was giving a class on atomic warfare to a group of basic trainees. Toward the end, he asked the class what the difference was between "radiation" and "contamination."

One "boot" straight from the farm piped up, "Well, sir, 'radiation' is when you smell manure; 'contamination' is when you step in it."

80.60

The army cook, after breaking hundreds of eggs to scramble for his hungry men, wearily sank into a chair and began a letter to his sweetheart back home. "Darling," he began, "for the last four hours, shells have been bursting all around me."

80.61

An Ontario sign spotter reports something new added to a recruiting poster, stating that "The Navy Builds Men!" Under it, in a feminine hand, was written, "Please build us each one! Mary, Susan, Joan."

80.62

Two privates in the army were puzzled by the carcass of a dead animal they found by the side of the road. One said, "It seems to have two stripes."

"That settles the whole thing. It's either a skunk or a corporal," said his friend.

80.63

Thus far, the whole rigmarole over an all-volunteer army has only come up with one concrete proposal: a way to solve veterans' housing. It's called "reenlistment."

80.64

Experts say an all-volunteer army will never work. Oh, no? What about the Salvation?

80.65

The major looked up from his desk and said to the private first class: "Now really, man, I ask you, if you were still in civilian life would you come to me with a puny complaint like this?"

"No, sir," he answered, "I'd send for you."

80.66

A milkman got drafted, and wrote back home: "I sure do like this man's army. It's really great to stay in bed till quarter to five."

80.67

A young private watched an old sergeant on his way to the Noncommissioned Officers Club. "There," he observed, "goes a bottle-scarred veteran."

80.68

The army is going to use TV commercials to popularize recruiting. It'll be known as: Operation Atsa Some Spicy Cannonball!

ART

86.50

An American in Paris met Pablo Picasso, and told him that he didn't like modern art because it wasn't representative of reality. Picasso said nothing. A few minutes later the man showed him a picture of his wife.

Said Picasso, "Is she really that small?"

86.51

The school teacher was taking her class through the Tate Gallery in London. "With a single stroke of the brush," she said, pointing to a portrait by Sir Joshua Reynolds, "Reynolds could change a smile to a frown."

"So can my mum," said a small Cockney lad.

86.52

A little old lady was touring an art gallery, and stopped to look at a piece of modern abstract painting. Noting her quizzical expression, the artist, who was standing nearby, said, "It is supposed to be a barn with horses in it."

The little lady replied, "Then why isn't it?"

86.53

The purchasing agent was showing a visiting salesman some of the modern painting his daughter had done. He pointed out one in particular which he proudly proclaimed was a gorgeous sunset. The salesman, anxious to put the proper enthusiasm in his reply, was nevertheless at a loss of words as he studied and restudied the atrocious brilliant-colored paint spatterings. As the silence lengthened, the proud father added, "She studied abroad, you know."

"Ah, that explains it," said the salesman in obvious relief. "I knew I had never seen anything like that called a sunset in this country."

86.54

When the artist's nude model arrived for her daily posing, he said, "Don't disrobe today. I don't feel like painting. Why don't you pour us both a drink instead?" Happily, the model did just that and settled comfortably on the couch beside the painter. After a few relaxed moments, they heard footsteps approaching the door. "Quick," exclaimed the artist. "It's my wife. Get your clothes off!"

86.55

"Cameos and small portraits do absolutely nothing for me. I like the scope and grandeur of huge, sweeping paintings."

"You an art critic?"

"No, a frame maker."

ATTITUDES

96.50

An optimist is a guy who sits in the last row of the burlesque and winks at the girls.

96.51

Sour grapes have upset a lot of apple carts.

96.52

Blessed is he who expects nothing for he shall never be disappointed.

96.53

The great Sam Levenson was being bugged by a heckler; he turned to the man and said, "Turn your glasses around and walk into yourself."

96.54

A good executive hires optimists for salesmen—and a pessimist for the credit manager.

96.55

Optimist: A fellow who grabs a fishing pole when he discovers that his basement is flooded.

96.56

A famous civil rights leader once shocked a group of his followers by saying that if he ever needed a heart or brain transplant, he would want the heart or brain of a bigot.

Asked for an explanation, he said, "Simple. I'd want one that had never been used."

96.57

A pessimist is a woman who thinks she can't park her car in a tiny space. An optimist is a man who thinks she won't try it.

96.58

Pessimist: One who doesn't waste time worrying because he knows everything will turn out wrong anyway.

96.59

Tolerance: The uncomfortable suspicion that the person you're talking to may be right.

96.60

Charity—The pasteurized milk of human kindness.

96.61

One thing you can say about an egoist—at least he never goes around talking about other people.

BEHAVIOR

110.50

A phony is a guy who tries to cut his throat with an electric razor.

110.51

An efficiency expert is someone who makes a foursome before going through a revolving door.

110.52

The parents of a young man who just announced that he had become a homosexual were perplexed.

"I can't understand it," said the father, "when he was baby we always dressed him in blue."

110.53

Diplomacy—The art of being able to say "Nice little doggie" until you have time to locate a rock.

110.54

A man who trims himself to suit everybody will soon whittle himself away.

110.55

Adult: A person who hasn't got enough nerve to walk down the street sucking a lollipop.

110.56

Wife: "Your behavior at the flower show was disgraceful." Husband: "I did the only thing I could do. I got potted."

110.57

Wolf—An individual who enjoys life, liberty and the happiness of pursuit.

110.58

You do not lead by hitting people over the head—that's assault, not leadership.

110.59

It is said that man has 12 million brain cells. In an urgent crisis, as a last resort, he will rely on about a dozen of them.

110.60

There's no fool like an old fool! You can't beat having all that experience.

110.61

What makes resisting temptation difficult for many people is that they don't want to discourage it completely.

110.62

To be exactly the opposite is also a form of imitation.

110.63

Husband to wife during argument: "Don't act like a fool!" Wife: "Do you want a monopoly on everything?"

110.64

If at first you *do* succeed, try to hide your astonishment.

110.65

I don't know what I'd do without my wife (girl) . . . I've never had the chance to find out.

110.66

"See that boy over there bothering Lila?"
"Ah, come on. He isn't even looking at her."
"I know. That's what's bothering her."

110.67

The test of a man or woman's breeding is how they behave in a quarrel.

110.68

The surest way to puncture a pleasure at its occurrence is to overanticipate it; the best things in life are not free, but unexpected.

BOOKS

120.50

A man returned for credit a book entitled, "How to Be Master in Your Own Home," and explained sheepishly, "My wife won't let me keep it."

120.51

On his way home one day, a recently married young man spied a book entitled "Forty Ways of Mating." He hurried in and bought the book without a second glance. While giving him his change, the clerk remarked, "I don't understand the sudden popularity of this book. It's outselling all our others, and I didn't even know so many people played chess."

120.52

"Do you know how to run a bookstore?"

"No sir, I don't have the slightest idea."

"In that case you're hired. You sound like you've had some experience."

120.53

"When does a book become a classic?" asked the teacher.

"When people who haven't read it begin saying they have," answered a smart student.

120.54

A hopeful writer sent a manuscript to a publisher with a letter stating, "The characters in this story are purely fictional, and bear no resemblance to any real people, living or dead."

The publisher wired back: "That's what is wrong with it."

120.55

The friends of a pompous rare book collector had had just about enough of the man's windy expertise, and decided on revenge. They hired an actor and introduced him as a country lawyer from Kansas. The conversation, as always, turned quickly to rare books.

"Me, I can't stand the smell of the moldy old books," said the alleged attorney. "A couple of days ago I threw out an old German bible that had been in the family for generations, I reckon."

"German bible you say. You don't remember offhand who printed it, do you?" asked the collector.

"I think it was Guten-somebody," the actor said.

"Not GUTENBERG!" shouted the collector. "You boob, you've thrown away a fortune. We've got to get back to Kansas and get it before it is destroyed!"

"Hang on," said the actor. "That bible can't be worth anything, Gutenberg or not. Some character named Luther scribbled his name all over it."

120.56

Humorist P. G. Wodehouse once dedicated one of his books to his wife and daughter thusly: "To my wife and daughter, without whose unfailing help and advice this book could have been written in half the time."

120.57

"You have a nice collection of books, but you really ought to have more shelves," said one friend to another.

"I know, but no one ever lends me shelves," was the answer.

120.58

The most absent-minded of all absent-minded professors was the one who forgot to write a $13.50 textbook to sell to his class.

BUSINESS
BUSINESSMEN

132.50

My sister-in-law's brother had to postpone the grand opening of his new midtown Manhattan store. The "Going out of Business" signs didn't arrive in time.

132.51

"I owe my success to Honesty and Wisdom," said the rich businessman to his son. "Honesty means that when you promise a customer something, you go through Hell and high water to deliver it—no matter the cost!"

"And what's Wisdom?" asked the son.

"Never promise a damn thing," said the father.

132.52

After the wedding ceremony of a businessman, he removed the "Just Married" sign from the back of his car and replaced it with a sign which read: "Under New Management."

132.53

A businessman has this sign under the glass top of his desk: "My decision is maybe—and that's final!"

132.54

A businessman was queried about his feelings toward a competitor up the street.

"There's nothing in the world I wouldn't do for Bill Johnson," he said, "and there's nothing he wouldn't do for me. That's the way we are. We go through life doing nothing for each other."

132.55

"So you want to know about business ethics," said the clothier to his son. "It's like this. The other day a customer comes in to clear up his account and hands me a $100 bill. After he left, I noticed there were two bills stuck together —$200. Now comes the question of business ethics. Should I tell my partner?"

132.56

The folly of human nature is neatly summed up by the case of the middle-aged teacher who invested her life savings in a business enterprise which had been elaborately explained to her by a swindler. When her investment disappeared and the wonderful dream was shattered, she went to the office of the Better Business Bureau.

"Why on earth," asked the man, "didn't you come to us first? Didn't you know about the Better Business Bureau?"

"Oh, yes," said the lady sadly, "I've always known about you. But I didn't come because I was afraid you'd tell me not to do it."

132.57

Our corner bakery is very successful because it operates on sound business principles—big profits, small turnovers.

132.58

Big Businessman Jones died and went straight down below. Things weren't too bad until he felt a tap on his shoulder and turned around to face the peskiest salesman he had ever known.

"Okay, Mr. Jones," boomed the salesman, "I'm ready for our appointment."

"Appointment? What appointment?"

"Don't you remember?" said the salesman. "Whenever I came to call on you up there you always told me you'd see me in hell first!"

132.59

I put a new product on the market and lost everything I had ... A week later the Russians invented it ... two weeks later the Japanese were selling it cheaper.

132.60

Two businessmen were discussing how they had achieved success. "Things were pretty tough for me for awhile," admitted one, "but I just gritted my teeth, rolled up my sleeves, and borrowed another $10,000 from my father-in-law."

132.61

Salesman: "These are especially strong shirts, madam. They simply laugh at the laundry."

Customer: "I know that kind. I had some which came back with their sides split."

132.62

If at first you do succeed, it's probably your father's business.

CARS
DRIVING

140.30

Policeman (pulling motorist over): "Excuse me, sir, but your left headlight seems to have gone out."

Motorist: Thank you, officer, but it doesn't matter that much."

Policeman: "It certainly does. How are your brakes?"

Motorist: "Lousy."

Policeman: "Could I see your license?"

Motorist: "I don't have one."

Policeman: "Well, that's three offenses. I'm going to have to arrest you."

Motorist's wife: "Oh, don't pay any attention to him, officer. He always talks this way when he's been drinking."

140.31

Owner of a foreign car repair shop: "When I was a boy my highest ambition was to be a pirate."

Client: "Congratulations."

140.32

Minister to mechanic: "Your estimate runneth over."

140.33

The head of a party vacancy committee was holding forth at a committee meeting. "We need a man who will drive on straight to his goal, looking neither to the right nor the left; one who presses forward and neither friend nor foe can delay him from his achievements. All who cross his path will do so at their own risk. Where, oh, where can we find such a man?"

From the back of the room came, "Driving the school bus."

140.34

A railroad claim agent was teaching his wife to drive, when the brakes let go on a steep, downhill grade. "What'll I do?" she shrilled.

"Brace yourself," he advised, "and try to hit something cheap."

140.35

A man's curiosity was aroused as he drove along a back road in the West and saw an Indian lying along the road with his ear to the ground. He stopped his car, walked over to the Indian and heard him say: "Small wheels, Pontiac, color blue, lady driving, two kids in back with large dog, Nebraska license plate."

"Amazing!" said the man observing the Indian. "You mean to say you can tell all that by putting your ear to the road?"

The Indian looked up in total disgust. "Ear nothing," he grunted. "That car ran over me ten minutes ago."

140.36

My daughter takes after her mother. We gave her a trip to Europe last summer. She came back and said, "Everybody's loaded over there. Almost everyone has a foreign car."

140.37

My uncle used to be a Texas magician ... he sawed a Cadillac in half.

140.38

A friend of mine was crossing the street last week, and was almost run down by a lady driving a station wagon full of kids. The lady had run a stop sign, so my friend shouted, "Lady, don't you know when to stop?"

And the lady said, "They're not all mine."

140.39

My car's tires are from France, its engine is from Germany, the body is from Detroit, and the transmission is from England. Isn't it wonderful that so many people can make a living from something that I haven't paid for yet?

140.40

A supernumary was being examined by the police chief for a regular position. The chief asked him, "If you were in a patrol car by yourself and were being pursued down a lonely country road by a gang of desperate criminals doing 70 miles an hour, what would you do?"

"Eighty," came the prompt response.

140.41

They've got a new car on the market ... it goes 160 mph, and stops on a dime ... then a putty knife comes out of the dashboard, and scrapes you off the windshield.

140.42

Our parking lot attendant is celebrating his eighth year on the job ... by getting his driver's license.

140.43

"Can I help you?" the Rolls-Royce salesman asked the Texan.

"Yep," was the reply. "My girl friend ain't feelin' well. What you got in the way of a get-well car?"

140.44

Prospect being given a demonstration ride in a used car:
    "Say, what makes it jerk when you put it in gear?"
Salesman: "Ah, that proves it's a good automobile. "It's anxious to get started."

140.45

A woman offered a brand-new Porsche for sale for a price of $10. A man answered the ad, but he was slightly disbelieving.

"What's the gimmick?" he inquired.

"No gimmick," the woman answered. "My husband died, and in his will he asked that the car be sold and the money go to his secretary."

140.46

When he was campaigning for the vice-presidency in 1968, Senator Edmund Muskie told the story of the Texas rancher who was bragging to the Maine farmer. The rancher said, "My ranch is so big that it takes me five whole days just to drive around the outside of it."

To which the Maine man replied, "Know what you mean. I've got a car like that, too."

140.47

A friend of mine has two complaints about his car: The motor won't start and the payments won't stop.

140.48

A man in the automobile business, asked a young lady what her neighbors would think if he were forced to reclaim her newly bought but, as yet, unpaid-for car.

The girl wrote back, "I have spoken with my neighbors as you suggested, and they think that it would be a lousy trick."

140.49

"Motorman," asked a rather stuffy woman, "at which end might I exit the car?"

The motorman replied, "Either one, sweets, they both stop."

140.50

A man driving in southern Indiana saw a sign which read: "Last chance for 32-cent gas." He stopped in and, as he was getting his change, he asked the attendant: "How much is gas in Kentucky?"

"Twenty-eight cents," he replied.

140.51

Used-car dealer (driving lemon): "This car represents the opportunity of a lifetime."

Customer: "Yeah, I can hear it knocking."

140.52

My mother-in-law told me she solved the parking problem—she bought a parked car.

140.53

My brother-in-law lived in a tough neighborhood and belonged to a very unusual car pool—every third week he had to steal one.

140.54

If your wife wants to learn to drive, don't stand in her way.

140.55

Paying the repair bills on a used car is a case of a lemon putting the squeeze on you!

140.56

You can always tell out-of-town cars in Los Angeles . . . they're the ones with fenders.

140.57

A friend says that there is one thing he has always been curious about: What does a nudist do with his car keys after he locks the car?

140.58

The experts say that there will be more than 300 million automobiles in use by the year 1980. So everybody that wants to cross the street had better do it now.

140.59

My new car has the engine in the rear ... of course, before my wife (girl) drove it, it had the engine in the front.

140.60

A policeman working on a bank robbery radioed in and said, "I've got a positive identification of the getaway car. It's either a '63, '64, '65, or '67 Volkswagen."

140.61

Policeman: "You were going at least 80 miles per hour."
Motorist: "How could you tell? I've only been on the road for 15 minutes."

140.62

Chauffeur: A New Yorker clever enough to drive an automobile but smart enough not to own one.

140.63

Natives who beat drums to ward off evil spirits are looked down upon by intellectual American drivers who blow horns to break up traffic jams.

140.64

Motorcycle policeman alongside speeding driver: "I'm only doing 75—how much are you only doing?"

140.65

Sign on the back of a truck: "Please don't hug me. I'm going steady."

140.66

Executive Ed proudly told a business friend how he cured his son of tardiness at school.

"I bought him a car," said Ed. "Now he has to get to school early in order to find a parking space."

140.67

Motorist—a person who, after seeing a horrendous wreck, drives safely for several blocks.

CHILDREN

152.30

A lovely widow and her six-year-old son were at a pool in Reno when a handsome stranger walked up and sat near them.

Suddenly the boy walked over to the man, and asked him his age, occupation, whether he was with anyone, and how long he was going to stay. Then he shouted to his mother, "Is there anything else you want me to ask him, Mom?"

152.31

Bill Cosby said that since he has become a parent, he's thrown all his child psychology books out the window. He said, "Give me 200 two-year-olds and I could take over any country in the world. Without anyone telling them anything, they know exactly how to shut off the power in your house, flood it out, and set fire to it."

152.32

During one of the many earthquakes scares in California, a couple sent their child to live with relatives in New York.

After three days, the California couple received a wire. It read: "Am returning the kid. Send quake."

152.33

School days can be the happiest of all—provided your kids are old enough to go.

152.34

The greatest influence on a child begins with the birth of his parents.

152.35

Three small boys entered a feed shop in a small village. The owner asked the smallest of the boys, "What do you want?"

"A box of copper brads," he replied.

The old man went up his ladder, brought down the box that contained the brads, took out a box, and reclimbed the ladder, putting away the box. Then he asked the second lad, "What can I get you?"

"A box of copper brads," he replied meekly.

"Why in tarnation didn't you say so before?" the old shopkeeper asked irritably.

He went up the ladder again, brought the box down, but before returning it, he asked the third boy, "Do you want a box of wire brads too?"

"No, sir," the boy replied.

The old man returned the box, and asked, "What can I get you?"

"Two boxes of wire brads, please!"

152.36

My son came in crying one day and said that one of the neighbor's kids had been throwing rocks at him, so he threw them back, and finally got beaned.

So my wife said, "Why didn't you tell me instead of throwing them back?"

The boy said, "What good would that do? You couldn't hit the broad side of a barn."

152.37

At the country estate of a distinguished publishing executive a small boy's head appeared over the fence and a meek voice asked, "Please, sir, could I have my arrow back?"

"Certainly, my boy," the executive replied. "Where is it?"

"I think," said the small boy, "that it's stuck in one of your cats."

152.38

John Smith telephoned a customer about an overdue account. A little girl answered.

"Is your mother home?" asked John.

"No," said the youngster.

"When will she be home?" John queried.

"Just a minute please," came the child's reply. "I'll ask her."

152.39

A little boy was gazing into the crib at his new baby sister who was lying there crying her head off.

"Did she come from Heaven?" the lad asked his mother.

"Yes," said the mother tenderly, "she did."

"Well, with all that noise she's making," said the little boy, "it's no wonder they threw her out."

152.40

"Mommy, come quick! I've hurt my toe."

"Which one, dear?"

"My youngest one."

152.41

"Why did you hit your brother in the stomach?" a mother inquired of her oldest.

The youngster replied, "Because he turned around."

152.42

In the bakery, the proprietor's small daughter stood guard behind the cream-puff counter.

"Aren't you tempted to eat them?" asked a solicitous customer.

"Of course not!" replied the tot with dignity. "That would be stealing. I only lick them."

152.43

I had a very happy childhood ... I never remember my father hitting me ... except in self-defense.

152.44

My brother-in-law said he was never going to fight again after the fights he had when he was a kid. Some of the other kids in the block would bet on him, and if he lost, they'd beat him up.

152.45

Man at door: "I'm asking for donations for the new children's home we're building. I hope you'll give what you can."

Tired-looking mother: "I'll give you two children."

152.46

The irritated mother was trying to find out why her five-year-old son had been punished in kindergarten for putting mud in a little girl's mouth.

"Why on earth did you do it?" she asked.

"Well," reasoned the boy, "it was open!"

152.47

A man walks into a hotel and says, "Do you take children?"

The clerk replies, "No, only cash or traveler's checks."

152.48

"Now, Johnnie," explained his mother, "you can't have the heavy hammer to play with. You'll hit your fingers."

"Oh no I won't," said Johnnie. "George is going to hold the nails."

152.49

A little boy had been pawing over a stationer's stock of greeting cards for some time when a clerk asked, "Just what is it you're looking for, sonny? Birthday greeting? Message to a sick friend?"

The boy shook his head "no" and answered wistfully, "Got anything in the line of blank report cards?"

152.50

"There will be a very small PTA meeting tomorrow night," the little tot sheepishly told his mother. "It's just you, me, and the teacher."

152.51

A young child was taken to see Santa Claus in a department store, and promptly walked up and kicked him in the shin. "That's for last year," said the toddler.

152.52

Here's a picture of me when I was only three hours old . . . in the background you can see my mother arguing with the doctor.

152.53

"Daddy?"

"What now, son?"

"Why didn't Noah swat both flies when he had the chance?"

152.54

Mother (to waitress): "Please wrap up this steak for the dog."

Little daughter: "Oh, boy, we're gonna get a dog!"

152.55

Robert Benchley said he saved everything as a child. He added, "I was rummaging through my bureau drawer once and came across some old snow."

152.56

"I've got 12 kids," said the distraught woman to the marriage counselor, "and I just found out my husband never loved me."

"You're lucky" he said, "just imagine how many kids you'd have if he did."

152.57

This Western craze has gone too far . . . the other day I saw a lady carrying her baby in a holster.

152.58

A loving mother, replying to a letter from the camp director who insisted her darling boy needed discipline, wrote: "Dear Sir: Please don't hit Seymour. Hit the boy next to him. That will scare Seymour."

152.59

As a child, I was the type of boy that my mother forbid me to play with.

152.60

Babies: Little knots in the bonds of matrimony.

152.61

Insanity is hereditary—parents get it from their children.

152.62

"I just came back from a pleasure trip."
"Where'd you go?"
"I drove my kids to camp."

152.63

Little boy: "My dad can beat up your dad."
Friend: "Big deal. So can my mother."

152.64

Childhood and genius have the same master organ in common—inquisitiveness.

152.65

All her life, my mother wanted children ... four years after I was born, she had her first child.

CITIES
CITY LIVING

156.50

A New York tycoon was visiting Salt Lake City. Strolling about town, he made the acquaintance of a little Mormon girl.

"I'm from New York," said the man. "I bet you don't even know where that is."

"Oh, yes," said the girl. "My Sunday school has a mission there."

156.51

From a well-to-do borough of New York, the governor's office received a letter complaining that its water supply was critical.

A governor's aide made light of it saying, "Those spoiled so-and-so's are always complaining they haven't enough water."

"This time," said another aide, "I think it's genuine. Their postage stamp is attached with a pin."

156.52

A city youngster, roaming around the country, found a pile of empty condensed milk cans. "Hey, guys," he called excitedly, "come here quick, I have found a cow's nest."

156.53

Al Smith, the happy warrior, started in the slums in lower Manhattan and became governor of New York and a candidate for the presidency. But he never forgot his humble origins. Once he was asked what degree he held, and he replied, "FFM."

"Which one is that?" asked the interrogator.

"Fulton Fish Market," said the governor.

156.54

A Brooklyn cabbie was skirting in and out of traffic with characteristic reckless abandon. After a few blocks, his harried passenger implored: "Please be more careful. I have nine children at home."

The driver turned slightly and said, "And you're tellin' me to be careful?"

156.55

A farmer and his wife sold the farm and moved to the city to retire. Early the first morning in their new home, the wife said, "Henry, isn't it about time you started the fire?"

"No, I don't believe I will," he answered. "It's about time we got used to some of these big city conveniences. I'm going to call the Fire Department."

156.56

If you're in California and you feel a tremor, there are two things to remember. Number One: Run to a doorway for safety. Number Two: The doorway should be in New York!

156.57

On a lonely New York street, a man heard a voice from the darkness: "Would the gentleman be so merciful and kind as to help a fellow who has had bad times? I don't have a thing in this world or the next except for this revolver."

156.58

Living in Los Angeles is a moving experience.

156.59

Talk about tough neighborhoods. At P.S. 1044, our school newspaper had an obituary page.

156.60

A little girl's family was moving to New York, and she was more than slightly displeased about it. But she knew that there was nothing she could do about it. So, at the end of her evening prayers, she said, "This is good-bye, God. We're moving to New York."

156.61

My daughter is a city girl. That's the only way I can explain it. I took her fishing with me the other day, and after two hours she threw her rod down and said she quit. I asked her why and she said, "Because, Daddy, I just can't seem to get waited on."

156.62

A bum on the street asked a man for 30 cents for a cup of coffee. The man replied, "I thought coffee was 15 cents."

The bum replied, "It is, but I've got a date."

156.63

Boy, did I live in a rough neighborhood as a child. I remember my mom giving my dad a dollar each morning for the holdup man.

156.64

Two sweet little old ladies from New York were touring Boston a few years ago, and one said to the other, "What do you think of Henry Cabot Lodge?"

Her friend replied, "I think I prefer Grossinger's."

156.65

People in New York are not basically rude—they are just afraid of being mistaken for visitors.

156.66

"Country air?" questioned a New Yorker with disbelief. "I like the air right here that you can sink your teeth into."

156.67

Talk about a tough neighborhood. Even the police station had a peephole in the front door.

CLOTHES
FASHION

168.50
Fastidious dresser: Someone who puts shoe trees in his tennis shoes.

168.51
A blushing bride had some bad news for her husband when he arrived home from the office. "I feel terrible," she sobbed, "I was pressing your best gray suit and burned a hole in the seat of the trousers."

"Think nothing of it," he replied gallantly. "I have another pair of trousers to that suit."

"I know and it's a good thing," she said, "I was able to use them to patch the hole."

168.52
At a late summer fur sale, a woman asked the furrier: "Will a small deposit hold this coat until my husband does something rotten?"

168.53
Milliner: "Excuse me madame. This is the hat in my hands, that's the box you're trying on."

168.54
The gorgeous receptionist was telling the rest of the girls in the office about her adventures the night before with the boss. "Do you know," she said, "he took me up to his apartment and showed me a closet with 15 mink coats. And he let me have my pick!"

"And what did you have to do?" asked a skeptic.

"Not much," said the secretary, "just shorten the sleeves."

168.55

Just about the time you finish teaching your kids that a container can't hold more than its capacity, along comes a hefty woman in hot pants.

168.56

Two ladies were discussing the upcoming dance at the social club. "We're supposed to wear something that matches our husbands' hair, so I'm wearing black," said Mrs. Jones.

"My," said Mrs. Smith, "I had better not go."

168.57

"Is this coat waterproof?"

"You ever seen a mink with an umbrella?"

168.58

The latest thing in clothes is usually the woman you are waiting for.

168.59

Well, I'm wearing the same old suit again ... the Salvation Army refused it.

168.60

A salesman phoned the manager of a clothing store and said, "Great news, I just sold that horrendous looking purple and chartreuse suit."

The manager went over to the store a little later and found the salesman bandaged from head to toe. "What happened?" was his first question.

"The customer's seeing-eye dog didn't like the color," was his answer.

168.61

A wife's announcement that she was so sick of wearing rags that she had marched into a store and purchased 10 new dresses that day had her husband completely unnerved. "Ten!" shrieked the wounded husband. "What could anyone want with 10 new dresses?" The wife answered promptly, "Ten new hats."

168.62

Dorothy Parker was attending a fancy ball in New York once when a clumsy waiter spilled coffee all over her new French gown.

"Go," she commanded, "and never darken my Dior again."

168.63

A dying wife turned to her husband and said, "Give your secretary my Paris dresses, my jewels, my furs."

He replied, "I can't, you're a size 16 and she's a 10."

168.64

Robert Fulton might have been talking about the mini skirt when he got his steamboat ready and said, "Well, now we won't have to wait for the wind."

168.65

We know a girl who was chased out of a nudist colony because she had something on her mind.

168.66

Boy, am I happy! I feel like a changed man . . . my laundry came back today.

168.67

This is some suit I got . . . yesterday it shrunk 4 inches . . . and it was only partly cloudy.

168.68

"Whenever I'm down in the dumps, I buy a new hat."
"I wondered where you got them."

168.69

Didja hear about the poor midget that wore hand-me-ups?

168.70

I've had this suit so long that it's been in style seven times since I bought it.

168.71

The micro skirt has a tendency to make men polite. No man ever got on a bus ahead of one.

CLUBS

170.50

"My dad is an Elk, a Moose, an Eagle, and a Lion," bragged one little lad.

"Gee," said his friend, "how much does it cost to see him?"

170.51

"Where did you get that black eye?"

"I went to a social club and was struck by the beauty of the place."

170.52

A friend of mine said he is now a confirmed bachelor. He sent his picture to the lonely hearts club, and they wrote back and said they weren't that lonely.

170.53

Times are changing. When a man gets mad at his wife now, he goes to his club. In the old days he just reached for it.

170.54

A down-at-the-heels bum sauntered into a swank golf club to the complete horror of the members. The chairman of the greens asked him rather politely to leave, but the tramp continued to stroll around the links. Several other members flared up when the interloper refused to heed their command to take off. Finally, the chairman could stand it no longer. He punched the bum in the nose, kicked him in the shins, grabbed him by the seat of the pants, and hurled him clean over a hedge. The bum picked himself up, brushed himself off, and calmly said: "Boy, that's one hell of a way to get new members!"

COMMUNICATIONS

180.50

A bachelor was grabbing a quick breakfast in an old roadside cafe one morning when he noticed an inscription on the side of an egg. It read, "If some nice young man who would like to marry a farmer's daughter reads this, write . . . "

The fellow quickly sent off a note, and four days later got his reply: "Your letter was too late. I'm now married and have four children."

180.51

This new semiprivate postal system is great. Now a letter posted before noon will be delivered the next morning—give or take a week.

180.52

The two business tycoons were discussing the antidiscrimination labor regulations. "I just can't understand it," said one. "Whoever wrote those regulations obviously never worked with women. Why, whenever I try to treat them like men, they break into tears. And when I try to treat them like women, my wife always finds out."

180.53

The salesman's son at college ended his fourth plea for more money with the words: "How can you call yourself a kind father when you haven't sent me a check for such a long time? Here I am practically starving. What kind of kindness do you call that?"

The father promptly sent off a telegram which read: "The answer to your last letter should be obvious. I call it 'unremitting kindness'."

180.54

Memo writing was the pet project of the plant superintendent. He not only snowed everyone under with his own
memos, but insisted that everyone report every out-of-the-
ordinary event to him in writing. One morning a man burst
into his office bearing this message from a foreman: "Man
walked in front of moving forklift truck. Further details
later."

After an interminable 10 minutes, the follow-up arrived:
"Everything O.K.," it read. "Forklift was moving back-
ward."

180.55

The telephone has a zillion uses, among which are the
"dial-a-service" facilities. You can dial the time, dial a
menu and, of course, dial a prayer. But I think there ought
to be a dial-a-prayer service for atheists. Of course, no one
would answer.

180.56

Having a young child explain something exciting he has
seen is the finest example of communication you will ever
hear or see.

180.57

A wife didn't know whether to get suspicious and ask for a
correction when the telegram from her conventioneering
husband read: "Having a wonderful time. Wish you were
her."

180.58

"You've got the wrong number," said the husband into the
phone. "You'll have to call the weather bureau."

"Who was that?" asked his wife.

"Some guy wanting to know if the coast was clear."

COUNTRY LIVING

202.50

The traveling salesman's car broke down one evening on a lonely road, and he asked at the only farmhouse in sight, "Can you put me up for the night?"

"I reckon I can," said the farmer, "but you'll have to share a room with my young son."

"How about that!" gasped the salesman, "I'm in the wrong joke!"

202.51

Dorothy Parker once visited the estate of some friends in the country, and became bored so quickly that she sent off a wire to another friend. It read: "Please send me a loaf of bread—and enclose a saw and file."

202.52

Movie attendance in the small town I'm from has never been too good. Last time I was home I called up and asked, "What time does the show start?"

And the lady said, "What time can you make it?"

202.53

An old Canadian guide had a green city man for a client, so he decided to break him to the backwoods life easily. So the first thing he asked the client was to go down to the stream and get a bucket of water. A few minutes later the man came bolting back to camp, white as snow, and without the bucket, and shrieked: "There was a bear in that stream!"

The experienced guide said, "Now, you've got to learn that that bear was just as scared of you as you were of it."

"Oh," the man said, relieved. "In that case the water wouldn't have been fit to drink anyway."

202.54
Hear about the small town that has had exactly the same population for 50 years? Every time a baby is born, a man leaves town.

202.55
First kid: "I'm gonna be a farmer."
Second kid: "You can't be a farmer."
First kid: "Why not?"
Second kid: "Because you don't have a daughter."

202.56
The owner of a small general store in Georgia was appointed postmaster for the area. For eight months, not a single piece of mail left his store. Concerned, the postal authorities in Washington wired him for an explanation.

They received this reply: "Bag ain't full yet."

202.57
Down-east storyteller Marshall Dodge tells of a tourist who stopped a Maine lobsterman and asked him, "Can I take this road to Portland?"

The lobsterman replied, "Shouldn't have to. They've got enough roads in Portland now."

202.58
The farmer took his son to the county fair. The boy watched with great interest and finally asked his father, "Pa, why does that man go around patting and pinching the cows?"

"He wants to buy one," said the father, "and he's trying to make sure he will get good meat."

A few days later, the boy raced out to the barn and yelled, "Hey, Pa, the postman is trying to buy Ma!"

202.59

A farmer was paying his first visit to a mental institution and came upon an inmate on the front lawn who was down on all fours watching the grass grow. As he stopped to watch the unfortunate fellow, the man raised up and said pleasantly, "My job is to watch the grass grow, what's yours?"

"Well, my job's not too different from yours," said the farmer tolerantly. "Except before I can watch things grow, I have to plow and plant the fields."

"Did you ever try being crazy?" asked the inmate.

"Why of course not," replied the farmer.

"It sure beats the hell out of farming," said the patient.

202.60

A young commuter, new to his route, was running to catch his train. He asked a farmer, "Do you mind if I take a shortcut through your field to catch the 6:45?"

"Not at all," he replied. "But if my bull sees you, you'll catch the 6:15."

202.61

Small town—Where everybody knows whose checks are good.

202.62

When a city slicker got stuck in the mud, a local farmer offered to help with his donkey. The mud was worse than it looked and it took a couple of hours of tugging and pulling to extricate the auto from the muck. When the farmer came back into the house, his wife looked at the muddy figure and asked, "How much did you get for all that work?"

"Two dollars," said the farmer.

"Only two dollars for all that hard work?" exclaimed the wife. "Sometimes, Pa, I wish you'd do the pullin' and let the other jackass handle the business end."

202.63

The tenderfoot from the East had spent all his time since arrival on the ranch asking all sorts of questions.

"Why is it?" he asked the cowboy, "that you always slap your horse on one side when you get in the saddle?"

"Well," said the cowpuncher, "I figure that if I can get one side started, the other is pretty sure to follow."

202.64

It was the salesman's first trip into the particular backwoods territory, and after a spine-jolting trip over rutted, potholed detours, he finally ended up in a small town garage to have a broken spring on his car repaired. In chatting with the mechanic, he remarked, "I'm sure glad that they're getting the roads around here fixed; I've never seen so many detours in my life. At least I won't have to worry about my springs on my next trip down here."

"Don't be too sure," replied the mechanic. "Whenever the road commissioner around here finds a real bad road, he just put, up a couple of signs calling the road a detour and lets it go at that."

202.65

Comedian Don Cooper said he lives in a town that is so small that it only has one Yellow Page. He said he tried to call home once and the area code was busy.

202.66

A traveling salesman stopped at a farm and asked, in the grand tradition, for lodging for the night. The farmer, true to form, told him he could sleep in the barn.

"Who lives here with you?" inquired the salesman.

"I live by myself," was the response.

The salesman replied angrily, "You mean to say you don't have three beautiful daughters, and you call yourself a farmer?"

202.67

My brother-in-law comes from a town that is so small that the barbershop quartet has only two people.

202.68

I'm just a farm boy who made good in the city. I've gone from the back 40 to the top 40 without ever losing my interest in corn.

202.69

I was born in a town that was so small that our telephone number was 9.

202.70

Small town: A place where, if you have a black eye, you don't have to explain it because everyone knows how you got it.

CRIME
CRIMINALS

208.40

Things had been quiet down at the precinct house, and some of the boys were playing cards to kill time. "What kind of a life is this?" asked one of the officers. "No riots, no strikes, no muggin's, no nothing."

"Be patient, Dan, things will pick up," said another, "you gotta have faith in human nature."

208.41

A genealogist had the unpleasant task of informing a sweet old client that an ancestor had been executed at Sing Sing.

He couldn't bring himself to use those words. When the lady walked in, he announced, "Mrs. Brownson, I have the pleasure to inform you that your great-great-uncle held the chair of applied electricity at one of our great public institutions."

208.42

A man raced up to the cockpit of a 727, pulled a gun and screamed, "Fly this thing to Miami."

The pilot, shocked, said, "You crazy idiot. That's where we were going anyway."

The man replied, "That's what you said last week."

208.43

An amateur soprano who sounded like a dying piece of sandpaper calling to its mate was singing a benefit at a prison.

The warden's son happened to be visiting his father that evening. After a few minutes of the performance, the warden turned to the boy and said, "Don, let this be a lesson to you if you are ever tempted to do wrong."

208.44

A prisoner about to go to the chair was asked what he would like for his last meal.

"Mushrooms," was his order.

"Sure thing," siad the guard, "but tell me. Why are you ordering mushrooms when you can have anything in the world?"

The prisoner said, "Because I've always been afraid to eat them."

208.45

The owner of a jewelry store called the police to report a robbery. "You won't believe this," said the man, "but a truck backed up to my window, then the back opened up, and an elephant stuck his trunk out. He broke the window, took all the watches and rings, pulled them into the truck, closed the truck door, and the truck took off."

The desk sergeant asked, "O.K., for identification purposes, was it an African elephant with big ears, or an Indian elephant with little ears?"

"I don't really know. He had a stocking over his head."

208.46

The coroner was addressing an eyewitness at the scene of a fatal shooting. "You mean to say the wife shot her husband with a pistol at close range?"

"Yes," said the witness.

"Were there powder marks on his face?"

"Yes; that's why she shot him."

208.47

Two men had burglarized a large home in the dead of winter, and were making their escape on the back of an ostrich. Looking over his shoulder at the tracks the bird was leaving in the snow, one of the pair said, "That ought to give the boys down at the crime lab something to think about."

208.48

Judge: "You say you burglarized this entire store by your-self?"

Defendant: "Yes, your honor. You can't trust anyone these days."

208.49

Two men on death row became good friends. But finally the day came for one's execution, and the other couldn't quite find the words to express his commiseration. Just as the first man was leaving for the electric chair, the other said, "Mike, more power to ya."

208.50

A man named Johnson broke into the home of a man named Wilson. He broke Wilson's arm and leg, stole his wife and car, took all the money, and burned the house to the ground.

When Wilson recovered, he began searching vengefully for Johnson. After years of going from town to town and following bum leads, he found him in a shack in the woods.

He burst in and shouted, "Johnson, you took my wife, stole my car and my money, and burned my house."

"So?" said Johnson.

"Well . . . cut that stuff out."

208.51

A famous dive near the Loop in Chicago was raided by police, and the guests and entertainers who hadn't escaped via the windows were hustled outside to the paddy wagon. The stellar attraction, Miss Veronica Verve, pushed every-one aside in her obvious desire to be the first into the wagon.

"What's the rush?" asked a cop.

"I know what I'm doing," replied Miss Verve. "The last four raids I had to stand!"

208.52

The incredible things women put in their handbags! Last week in New York's Central Park a juvenile snatched a purse and got $27 and a hernia.

208.53

The absentminded crook pulled a gun, walked up to the teller in a bank, and said, "Take me to Havana!"

208.54

A vaudeville comedian was deathly afraid of being robbed in the towns he traveled to. Arriving in his hotel room, he would nail the windows shut, put the bureau against the door, and turn out the light.

Then, for an extra touch, he would say into the darkness, "Well, Pittsburgh and broke again."

208.55

The detective arrived at the bank and said to the bank president, "I hear you're looking for your chief teller. Is he tall or short?"

The banker replied, "Both."

208.56

"Just what good have you done for humanity?" asked the judge before passing sentence on the pickpocket.

"Well," replied the confirmed criminal thoughtfully, "I've kept three or four detectives working regularly."

208.57

A hold-up man walked up to the teller and demanded the cash in small, unmarked bills. The teller replied, "The least you can do is smile. You're having your picture taken."

208.58

Judge, speaking to con man: "How could you swindle these good people who trusted you so?"

Defendant: "Your Honor, you can't swindle people who don't trust you!"

208.59

"Look, Mommy," urged the four-year-old, as she watched a prison riot on television, "there are some men fighting in their playpen."

208.60

A man came home in the wee hours and found a burglar picking the lock on the door. He said to the thief, "I'll open it if you'll go in first."

208.61

One thing you can say for the Cosa Nostra: They are one of the few groups that still make house calls.

208.62

In the immortal words of Al Capone, "You can get more with a kind word and a gun than just a kind word."

208.63

There is only one gift for the man who had everything—a burglar alarm.

208.64

Drug addiction is giving crime a shot in the arm.

208.65

Stork—A bird that takes the rap for many crimes that should be charged to a lark.

DOCTORS

232.30

Mike Halberian, owner and host of Knickers Pub, reports that the other evening a couple was having dinner there, when the wife's psychiatrist dropped in unexpectedly for a drink. Spotting her doctor at the bar, the lady ambled over to him and gushed, "What a lovely surprise to see you here, Doctor. You must come over and meet my husband. He's one of the men I mentioned to you on my last visit."

232.31

A cardiac patient was about to inherit a million dollars so, on the request of the man's wife, the family doctor agreed to be present when he was to get the news.

But everything went smoothly until the man said he was so happy that he was going to give the doctor half. The doctor dropped dead.

232.32

"Please forgive me for being late," said the young surgeon to his date, "but I had to perform an emergency appendectomy on a patient of mine."

"Really? What was wrong with him?"

232.33

A doctor vows that the chairman of a meeting of throat specialists in Philadelphia declared on the platform, "You have all heard the motion. All in favor say 'ah'."

232.34

One practical medical school gives the top five graduates in the class bunches of 10-year-old magazines so their patients won't think they are new in the business.

232.35

There's still no such thing in this country as a woman who is a doctor. She's still a "woman doctor."

232.36

An elderly woman called a doctor and sobbed into the phone, "Doctor, you might not remember me, but five years ago you told me to go home, go to bed, and stay there until you called. Well, you never called."

"I didn't?" the doctor said. "Then what are you doing out of bed?"

232.37

"Doctor, did you ever make a serious mistake?"

"Yes. Once I cured a multimillionaire in two visits."

232.38

A marketing executive was being offered a heart transplant. The surgeon suggested the heart of a young athlete or a salesman.

"If you don't mind," said the exec, "I'd rather wait for the heart of a mortgage banker, one that hasn't been used much."

232.39

A disheveled man raced into a psychiatrist's office, tore a cigar apart and stuffed the tobacco up his nose.

"Can I help?" asked the doctor.

"Yeah. Gotta light?"

232.40

"I certainly performed the operation in the nick of time," said the young doctor to a colleague, "another few hours and he would have recovered without it."

232.41

A woman walked into a psychiatrist's office leading a large white duck on a leash. "What can I do for you, madam?" asked the psychiatrist.

"It's not me that needs help, Doctor," said the woman. "It's my husband here. He thinks he's a duck."

232.42

My brother-in-law went to see a psychiatrist, and the doctor said to him: "Despite what you or your relatives think, you do not have a complex. You are inferior."

232.43

Doctor: "I'm sorry to tell you that your wife's mind is completely gone."

Husband: "I'm not surprised. She's been giving me pieces of it for 20 years."

232.44

After a successful recovery from a major operation, the tycoon returned to his doctor's office for a final checkup. After he was pronounced in perfect health, the doctor said, "Here's the bill for my services. You can pay $1,000 down and $100 a month for the next 24 months."

"Just like buying an automobile," remarked the patient. The doctor smiled and replied, "I am."

232.45

The doctor went right up to the patient's room, but came down a few moments later and asked for a chisel. He reappeared a minute later and asked for a can opener. Then he came and asked for a hammer and screwdriver. The distraught wife couldn't stand it anymore. "God, Doctor, you've got to tell me what's wrong with him."

"Don't know," said the physician, "can't get my bag open."

232.46

    Patient: "Doctor, what I need is something to stir me up—something to put me in fighting trim. Did you put anything like that in this prescription?"

Doctor: "No. You will find that in the bill."

232.47

A prominent society physician set out on a hunting trip one day but returned empty-handed. "I didn't kill a thing today," he admitted.

    "That's the first time that's happened in years," said his unfeeling wife.

232.48

    Dentist: "Could you pay for a full set of teeth if I found them necessary?"

Patient: "And if I couldn't pay, would they still be necessary?"

232.49

Virus—A Latin word used by doctors to mean "it could be anything."

232.50

There is nothing like a new ache or pain to make you pay an old doctor's bill.

232.51

    Doctor: "Is your flu any better?"

Country Bill: "Nope."

Doctor: "Did you drink the orange juice after the hot bath?"

Bill: "Nope. After drinking the hot bath I couldn't get the orange juice down."

232.52

"You told me last time that you were going to a psychiatrist," said the salesman to the purchasing agent. "Are you still seeing him regularly?"

"Nope," replied the purchasing agent. "I'm cured. I used to be terribly conceited, but my doctor straightened me out. Now I'm one of the nicest guys in town."

232.53

The psychiatrist said to his patient, "My good man, you are finally cured."

The patient dejectedly replied, "Some cure. When I came here I was King Richard the Lion-Hearted. Now I'm just another nobody."

232.54

Psychiatrist to office nurse: "Just say we're awfully busy—not 'It's a madhouse'."

232.55

"I'll see you in the morning," said the doctor to the critically ill patient.

"OK, Doc," said the patient, "but will I see you?"

232.56

In spite of the psychiatrist's assurances, his patient insisted he had swallowed a horse. Finally, in desperation, the psychiatrist agreed to "operate." He put the patient to sleep for a few moments, and before he woke up, the doctor led a horse into the operating room. As the patient opened his eyes, the psychiatrist pointed to the horse. "Well," he said, "that won't bother you any more."

The patient stared for a moment, and then sadly shook his head. "I don't know where you got that brown one from, Doctor, but the horse I swallowed was white."

232.57

Psychiatrist: "My man, do you have any trouble making decisions?"

Patient: "Well, yes and no."

232.58

Doctor: "I'll examine you for $10."

Patient: "Great. If you find it, I'll split it with you."

232.59

Taking a tranquilizer may not relax you, but it will make you enjoy being tense.

232.60

"Did the patient take his medicine religiously every time he was supposed to?"

"No, he swore every time he had to swallow it."

ECOLOGY

240.50

Two men were talking about ecology in a bar. One said, "Glass recycling is really going great. In fact, they're using some of the crushed glass in highway construction."

"Wonderful," said the other, "let's have one for the road."

240.51

If you're unfortunate enough not to have a dirty river in your area maybe something in air pollution would help. Think about it.

240.52

Pollution is affecting everything. Did you hear about the 98-pound weakling who took his girl friend to the beach—and a bully kicked oil in his face?

240.53

The (local) mayor cleaned up air pollution . . . now no one likes the taste.

240.54

Auto makers have been ordered to rid cars of exhaust fumes. There's so much smog over some cities that a guy can hardly find his way to hijack a plane.

240.55

The army recently admitted that deadly gases had been tested in the atmosphere. It was noted, however, that they had been tested over Los Angeles, so no one noticed.

240.56
"Why in heck are you three hours late?" screamed the boss.

"Because my wife went on an ecology kick," came the humble reply.

"Eh?" asked the boss incredulously.

"Yeah. She recycled my glasses."

240.57
One New Yorker said he could always tell when it was spring in the city. It was when the garbage went up the Hudson River to spawn.

240.58
Right after the government's ban on swordfish, a man went into a restaurant and ordered it. The waitress was in a good mood, so she shouted back to the kitchen, "Broiled swordfish, hold the mercury!"

240.59
Pollution is one of the things that everybody talks about and everybody does something about—like contributes to it.

240.60
The head of the sanitation department greeted his men one day with "Good morning, fellow ecologists!"

240.61
Man is a complex being; he makes deserts bloom—and lakes die.

240.62
The (local) river has just been rated X.

EDUCATION

246.50

The dean of the school wouldn't allow the star player to play in the big game coming up on Saturday. The coach brought the player into the dean's office and cried, "Why don't you let him play Saturday? We need him!"

"I'll tell you why," snapped the dean. "This is supposed to be a school of learning. All he knows is sports, and I'll show you how ignorant he is." Then turning to the player he said: "Tell me, how much is 14 divided by two?"

"Five," came the answer.

With that the coach cried to the dean, "Aw, let him play. After all, he only missed it by one."

246.51

At a recent New England town meeting, one irate mother rose and said, "I'm definitely opposed to sex education in the schools for my son, and I've felt that way ever since the stork brought him."

246.52

Teacher: "This report you wrote about your neighborhood is exactly the same as the one your brother did last year. In fact, it's word for word."
Student: "Well, it's the same neighborhood."

246.53

Teacher: "Which hand does the Statue of Liberty have over its head?"
Student: "The one with the torch."

246.54

Small boy, showing teacher's report card to his father: "Well, they're not paying her enough, for one thing!"

246.55

At a large Midwestern university, male students were moved into a wing of a previously all-girl dormitory. The male wing was parallel to the main section of the building.

Things went along as smoothly as could be expected until the girls' housemother noticed that the lads were keeping the shades open a little too often.

She sent a note over which read, "Course in anatomy not appreciated."

The boys quickly sent one back, "Course in anatomy optional."

246.56

College—A fountain of knowledge where students go to drink.

246.57

"If that klutz is a professor, then it would be smarter to watch daytime television. Everybody thinks he's too dumb to have gotten in here as a student. He can't explain anything, can't introduce new ideas, and ought to go back to the soap factory he came from."

"Yeah, he flunked me, too."

246.58

I wish I could have gone to college. Only one thing stopped me . . . high school!

246.59

"I'm sending you the $10 you requested in your last letter," wrote the businessman to his son at college. "However, I'm surprised that at your educational level you haven't learned to be more careful with your spelling. There was one error in your letter that I must call to your attention: The figure 10 is written with one nought, not two."

246.60

"Well," said the teacher, "there are a lot of reasons why you didn't get a higher mark on the test. For instance, your answer to the question 'Why did the pioneers strike off into the wilderness?' was interesting from the viewpoint of sanitation, but not really what I was looking for."

246.61

"Now can anybody tell me," asked the geography teacher, "where we find mangoes?"

"Yes, Miss," replied a knowing little boy, "wherever woman goes."

246.62

A father was passing through his son's college town, and decided to pay a surprise visit. Arriving at his son's dormitory at 3 a.m., he was at first unable to raise anybody.

Finally a voice came from the second floor: "Whaddaya want?"

The father shouted up, "Does Victor Dunham live here?"

"Yeah," came the answer, "carry him in."

246.63

The greatest educational dogma is also its greatest fallacy: the belief that what must be learned can necessarily be taught.

246.64

Mingling with the throng that poured out of California University stadium after a big game, a visiting Easterner enthused to his host, head of the chemistry department, "What a plant you have here! What a campus! How many students would you say you have?"

The chemistry professor answered sourly, "About one in a thousand."

246.65

"What do you expect from your college education?" a professor asked an extremely wealthy student.

The lad replied, "Well, I won't have to buy my stocks from strangers."

246.66

When the time comes that everyone in this country has a Ph.D., the last garbage man will make a fortune.

246.67

Most college campuses are crowded. If a student wants to be alone, he has to go to class.

246.68

Homework—Something teen-agers do between telephone calls.

246.69

Teacher: "What's a Grecian Urn?"
Student: "Oh, about a dollar an hour."

EMPLOYER
EMPLOYEE RELATIONS

256.50

The boss had a young employee on the carpet and was giving him a lecture on efficiency and devotion to duty. However, the employee answered by criticizing the way in which the company and the department was being managed. The boss angrily demanded, "Are you the boss of this department?"

"No, sir, of course not," said the employee.

"Well, then," thundered the boss, "don't talk like a fool!"

256.51

Client: "If there is something wrong with my performance on the job, don't give me a long scientific name for it. Tell me so I can understand."

Counselor: "All right, you're lazy and incompetent."

Client: "O.K., now give me the scientific name so I can tell my boss."

256.52

Office boy: "I think the phone is for you."

Manager: "Waddaya mean 'think it's for me'?"

Office boy: "The voice said: 'Is that you, you crazy old idiot?' "

256.53

A foreman rushed up to his contractor boss and shouted, "We just removed the scaffolding from the three new houses on 'K' Street and they collapsed in a heap." Gilligan investigated, and turned on the foreman in a rage. "How often do I have to tell you guys—never remove the scaffolding till the wallpaper's up!"

256.54

Really, you just can't help liking the boss here at (name of company). If you don't, he'll fire you!

256.55

"Who," bellowed the boss, "told you that just because I've kissed you a few times you could loaf around and not do any work?"

"My lawyer," burbled his secretary.

256.56

"I feel like punching the sales manager right in the mouth again."

"You mean you let him have it before?"

"No, I felt like letting him have it before."

256.57

"I know you can't get married on the money I'm paying you," said the boss to the eager new employee, "and some day you'll thank me for it."

256.58

"How long have you been working for the company?"

"Since the boss threatened to fire me."

256.59

Secretary to boss: "Certainly I have a good reason for being late. It makes the day seem shorter."

256.60

"You'll love it here," said the personnel director to the delicious new steno. "Lots of chances for advances."

256.61

"When I walk through the typist section, I feel like a piece of uranium approaching a whole battery of Geiger counters," commented the office manager to a friend.

"What do you mean?" asked the friend.

"Well, the closer I get, the faster the clicks."

256.62

An executive is the man who talks with visitors so the other employees can get their work done.

ENTERTAINMENT
ENTERTAINERS

266.40

A film star once saw another actor at a premiere with a beautiful girl on his arm. "That is his wife," someone said. "His wife!" the actor exclaimed, "that's what I call publicity."

266.41

An aspiring actor was trying to beat his rent for another month, and told his landlord, "In a few years, people will point with pride to this building and say, 'Johnston, the famous actor, used to live there'."

The landlord replied, "If I don't get the rent, they'll be saying it tomorrow."

266.42

Stage star to dentist: "It's the one in the front row, left, in the balcony."

266.43

They say that movie stars are all alike. That's ridiculous ... do you see any similarity between Raquel Welch and Lassie?

266.44

A couple went to the circus, and got there just as a trapeze artist was swinging by his toes hundreds of feet in the air.

The woman watched enraptured as the man swung back and forth, with no net to break the fall. Then she gasped as the man produced a fiddle and began playing behind his back.

"Isn't he marvelous?" shrieked the wife.

"Heifetz he ain't," said the husband.

266.45

An aging chorus girl was seated in a Hollywood restaurant when a famous star glided past and waved to her. "Gee," gushed an aspiring young actress at the same table, "Do you actually know her?"

"Honey," said the old-timer, "I knew her when she didn't know where her next husband was coming from."

266.46

The owner of the Ringling Brothers, Barnum & Bailey Circus reportedly moaned when he heard that the famous Mildred Zacchini, of the human cannonball family, was retiring. "Where," he complained, "are we going to get another woman of her caliber?"

266.47

The movie director was telling the actor, "The lion will chase you for exactly 100 yards, do you understand?"

"Yeah, I understand. But does he?"

266.48

The Academy Award nominations came out. For those of you unfamiliar with the Academy Awards—they're like a massage parlor for Hollywood egos.

266.49

Comedienne Phyllis Diller said that, when she played Post Office as a kid, she always ended up in the dead letter office. She said one of the reasons was that she was so skinny that when she put on a striped dress it only had one stripe.

266.50

I went into one movie that was so wild, the only one wearing clothes was the projectionist!

266.51
Playing a one-nighter in Flint, Michigan, comic pianist Victor Borge was undaunted by the fact that the house was less than half filled. Looking out at the sparse crowd, Borge said: "Flint must be an extremely wealthy town. I see that each of you bought two or three seats."

266.52
The budget's a little tight this week, so instead of a bubble dancer, we're gonna have a nude midget and a grape.

266.53
I saw a movie last night that was so good they're gonna make a book out of it.

266.54
Dick Cavett says he's normally very shy and retiring at parties. He said he just likes to sit in the corner and watch the avocado dip turn black.

266.55
Writer-actor Peter Ustinov says he gets a bit of ribbing about his beard, but is going to keep it anyway. He said, "People can hear me better when I talk above a whisker."

266.56
As usual, I don't agree with some of the Academy nominations. For instance, when it comes to Best Performance in a Supporting Role—what about Aristotle Onassis?

266.57
John Wayne was fantastic during the earthquake. The first thing he did was draw all of the houses into a circle!

266.58

There's a crisis in the movie industry: Nobody under eighteen can see the movies and nobody over forty can eat the popcorn.

266.59

I went to one of those new movies last week that was so bloody that it was rated "O-positive."

266.60

Fame is a seat on a ferris wheel.

266.61

A polling service accidentally discovered that most of the prisoners in a jail watched only daytime television. Curious, the head of the poll asked one prisoner why the men watched in the day and not the night.

The man told him the lights went out at 8:30 p.m., which precluded night viewing, and said the men watched in the day because they thought it was part of the punishment.

266.62

I was a pioneer in television, gang. They used my face for two years as the test pattern.

266.63

Isn't electricity GREAT! Just think, without it we would have to watch TV by candlelight!

266.64

I saw a modern TV Western last night ... the cowboy rolled a cigarette, and the girl rolled a drunk.

ETIQUETTE

276.50

A fat man and his wife were returning to their seats after the intermission.

"Pardon me," said the man to the man on the aisle, "but did I step on your toes on my way out?"

"Yes, as a matter of fact you did," the seated man said.

The obese one turned to his wife and said, "O.K., Harriet, this is our row."

276.51

Etiquette is knowing the proper two fingers to stick in your mouth when you whistle for the waiter.

276.52

Members of the school board were visiting classrooms to observe teachers and students at work. Afterward they met with the faculty to discuss the problems of modern teaching. "Are there any abnormal children in your class?" asked a board member of one particularly worn-looking teacher.

"Yes," replied the overworked one. "There are two with good manners."

276.53

A bird in the hand is bad table manners.

FACES
FACIAL

286.50

She had a face that men go for ... they used to call her "Gopher Face."

286.51

What a girl. I never forget a face, and in her case, I'll remember both of them.

286.52

Barber: "You've been in before? Funny, but I don't remember your face."
Customer: "No doubt. It has since healed."

286.53

My aunt is so ugly that starvation wouldn't even look her in the face.

286.54

Dimple: A ripple in the gentle whirlpool of a pretty girl's smile.

286.55

At a Hollywood premiere, a man rushed up to Groucho Marx and said, "Hey, Groucho! Remember me?"
    To which the comic replied, "I never forget a face, but in your case I'll make an exception."

FAMILY
FAMILY RELATIONS

294.30

A big-game hunter took his wife and mother-in-law on an African safari. One night, in the middle of the jungle, the couple awoke to find mother missing. They searched until dawn and finally found her in a clearing with a huge lion standing over her.

"Whatever are we going to do?" shrieked the wife.

"Nothing," said the husband, "the lion got himself into this, let him get himself out of it."

294.31

"Am I descended from an ape?" a small boy asked his mother.

"I don't know," she answered, "I never met your father's side of the family."

294.32

A miser is not much fun to live with, but he makes a great ancestor.

294.33

I'll never forget my graduation ... My parents didn't exactly ask me to strike out on my own, except in a subtle way ... like wrapping my lunch in roadmaps.

294.34

"I thought I told you not to tell mother how late I came in last night," shouted the young man at his sister.

"I didn't tell her what time you came in," she insisted. "I just said that I was too busy setting the breakfast table to notice the time."

294.35

Milton Berle once introduced the Father of the Year to his audience. The man had actually sired 27 children. The proud father confessed, "I'm pretty tired, I'm usually in bed by this time."

294.36

Two businessmen, meeting at lunch, were discussing their families. "I have 6 boys," one of them said.

"That's a nice family," sighed the other. "I wish to heaven I had 6 children."

"Don't you have any children?" the proud father asked with a touch of sympathy in his voice.

"Oh, yes," sighed the second man. "Twelve."

294.37

My uncle didn't exactly like his wife, so he had 18 kids . . . and lost himself in the crowd.

294.38

Wife on a boating excursion: "If the boat foundered, who would you save first, the children or me?"
Husband: "Me."

294.39

A credit manager showed up for work one morning and passed out jars of honey to all his co-workers. "Fresh from the hive," he announced proudly. "It's from the bees that I bought last year."

One of the other men was interested in learning more about the problems of keeping bees. "Don't they give you a lot of trouble?" he asked.

"Some," admitted the credit manager, "but it's well worth it. Besides the honey we get, the bees have already stung my mother-in-law five times."

294.40

As the young father wheeled his young identical twins through the park one day, the fifth woman in a row approached and made the usual absurd sounds. She then turned to the father and asked: "They're so cute. Are they twins?"

The young man looked her straight in the eye as he replied, "No, madam. I happen to have two wives."

294.41

Next time someone boasts to you of his long and ancient family lineage, remind him that the older the seed, the worse the crop.

294.42

First boy: "I heard you have a new brother."
Second boy: "Yes, he screams all the time. I can't sleep."
First boy: "Why don't you send him back?"
Second boy: "Can't. We've used him four days already."

294.43

"Could you donate something to the Old Ladies Home?"
   "Sure, I'll have my mother-in-law there in the morning."

294.44

A young father reached the ultimate the other night when he overheard himself yelling up the stairs: "OK. This is the last time I'm going to tell you kids for the last time!"

294.45

I just discovered that parenthood is hereditary ... if your parents didn't have any children, the chances are that you won't have any either.

294.46

The salesman one day approached his teen-age son and suggested, "Son, I think it's about time we had ourselves a man-to-man talk about the birds and the bees."

"O.K., Dad, but since I already know about that subject," said the youngster, "what do you say we discuss the car and the keys?"

294.47

I don't mind my wife's mother living with us, but I wish she'd quit using my shaving brush.

294.48

Two young boys in Hollywood were arguing. The first said, "My dad can beat up your dad."

His friend said, "Oh, yeh? Well, my dad is your dad."

294.49

When a woman wants her husband to start a garden, the first thing he usually digs up is a good excuse.

294.50

I took my girl to meet my parents two months ago. They loved her, but they still don't approve of me.

294.51

The jet-set husband phoned his wife from his office and said, "Darling, I'm overworked. Why don't we fly down to Bermuda for a couple of days?"

The wife was delighted. Then, in a very nice voice the husband said, "I really don't like to bring this up, luv, but couldn't we, just this once, leave your mother at home?"

"*My* mother," she shrieked. "Good Lord, I thought she was *your* mother."

294.52

I wouldn't say my mother was overfastidious. But when I got up to go to the bathroom in the middle of the night, by the time I got back the bed was made.

294.53

Mothers, if you're worn out and want a few minutes to yourself, do the dishes.

294.54

"Who are you working for these days?"
   "Same old people. My wife and five kids."

294.55

When I was five, my family moved ... but I found them again.

FINANCES
MONEY

302.01

A man met his tailor one day and asked him why he never sent him a bill. The tailor replied that he never asked a gentleman for money. The man then asked him what would happen if someone did not pay.

The tailor replied, "After a certain period of time, I would conclude that he was not a gentleman and ask him."

302.02

It is every man's ambition to be able to afford what he is spending.

302.03

When confronted by bills from the doctor and the electric company; a young man advised his wife to pay the electric company first. "After all," he explained, "the doctor can't shut off your blood."

302.04

The relatives were all gathered expectantly for the reading of wealthy Uncle Rodney's will. The lawyer opened the document and read, "Being of sound mind, I spent all my money."

302.05

The mistress was showing one of the neighbors around her house.

"This bureau," she said, "goes all the way back to Louis the Fourteenth."

"Don't feel bad," advised the neighbor, "my whole living room set goes back to the furniture store the fifteenth."

302.06

Sam Fink, president of Fink Co. and the most miserly boss who ever lived, finally died. At the funeral, six men carried Fink's casket out of the church when, suddenly, the lid opened and Fink himself popped up.

"If you put this casket on wheels," said Fink, "you could fire four men!"

302.07

The man who can think fast will go far. Take for example Texas Jack Garner, the former vice president. He lost a $10 bet on a Washington ball game and the winner asked him to autograph the bill so his grandson could have a souvenir.

"You mean he's not going to spend the money?" said Garner.

"That's right."

"In that case, I'll write you a check."

302.08

One of the most blatant dunnings came from a department store to one of its habitual deadbeats. The bill read, "Sir, you have been on our books for more than a year. We have carried you longer than your mother did."

302.09

Everyone these days is collecting for some kind of charity. A lady with a tin cup came up to my brother-in-law last week and asked him for a contribution. He asked her what it was for, and she told him it was for a fallen woman. So he said, "I always give direct."

302.10

Finance company's billboard pitch in Indianapolis, Indiana: "Now, you can borrow enough to get completely out of debt."

302.11

A new young resident visited her neighborhood super-market for the first time. Introducing herself to a young checker, she asked what the store's procedure was for cashing personal checks. He thought for a moment, then brightened.

"There's no special procedure, lady," he said kindly. "You just come in and let the manager get familiar with you."

302.12

A farmer, during a bank panic, balked at receiving a cashier's check when he tried to withdraw his savings. The bank president took him aside and tried to explain. As he finished his explanation, he asked, "You understand, don't you?"

"I think I do," admitted the farmer. "It's like this, isn't it? When my baby wakes up at night and wants some milk, I give him a milk ticket."

302.13

A business methods teacher, dragged out of her typing class and forced to teach accounting, explained to the class how she knew that the company she had invested in was prospering. "When I get the annual report, I add up the total assets and the total liabilities. If they're the same, then I figure that everything is all right."

302.14

Every Friday a friend of mine had to turn over his pay to his wife. Then she would give him a buck and half for cigars. But once he came home and screamed, "I did it! I won a lottery for 50 grand! You won't believe it, but I did it!"

"And where," she demanded, "did you get the money for the ticket?"

302.15

In the plush dining room of a private Wall Street club, several portly gentleman were discussing who the greatest inventor was. Was it Edison or Morse, Ford or Whitney? Finally an imperious financier broke in, "Well, the man who invented interest was no fool."

302.16

"Why did you get fired from your last job?" asked the personnel man.

"I was overly ambitious," replied the young applicant.

"How so?" asked the man.

"I took my work home with me."

"Who did you work for?"

"The First National Bank and Trust Company."

302.17

Pay television on a large scale is not all that new. The installment plan has been with us for years.

302.18

Money does make all the difference. If you have two jobs and you're rich, you have diversified interests. If you have two jobs and you're poor, you're moonlighting.

302.19

His last will and testament completed, the old man in the oxygen tent fondly told his son that all his wealth, stocks, bonds, bank account, and real estate would be his after the end finally came.

"Dad, Dad," whispered the weeping son, his voice emotion-choked, "I can't tell you how grateful I am ... how unworthy I am ... Is there ... is there ... anything I can do for you? Anything at all?"

"Well, Son," came the feeble reply, "I'd appreciate it very much if you took your foot off the oxygen hose."

302.20

A banker had just returned from a convention and turned in his expense account. He was called into the manager's office.

"This expense account amazes me," the manager said. "How did you manage to spend $15 a day on food?"

"I managed," came the reply, "by skipping breakfast."

302.21

Then there was the down-at-the-heels businessman who always dated his checks ahead. When he passed on, his creditors bought him a tombstone. It read: "Here lies Bruce Moskowitz. Died Oct. 31, as of May 10."

302.22

"And what is your name, sir?" a bank teller politely asked a customer.

The man shot back: "Can't you see my signature?"

The teller said: "Yes, and that's what piqued my curiosity."

302.23

My brother-in-law told me that bill collectors always come at the wrong time—when he's home.

302.24

My great-uncle was a notorious cheapskate. He cut all corners, then cut the circles. Saved everything. Always had to have the best bargain in town.

But there hadn't been a sale in months. Finally, he couldn't stand it anymore. He got a gun, went into a clothing store and said "Gimme a suit."

The clerk was more than obliging, and produced a $300 three-piece mohair suit.

So my man said, "Don't you have anything cheaper?"

302.25

Two bank tellers were counting packets of 100-thousand-dollar bills. One of them ripped the band off the first packet, started counting and, when he got to 62, he stopped, scooped up and grabbed another packet.

His friend inquired about his behavior, and he explained, "If it's all right that far, it's probably all right all the way."

302.26

A lady walked into an appliance store and asked to see some toasters. A high-pressure salesman decided instead to sell her an expensive freezer.

"Madam," he pitched, "believe me when I tell you this freezer will pay for itself in no time at all."

"Fine," said the lady. "As soon as it does, send it over."

302.27

Money doesn't always buy happiness. A man with 20 million isn't that much happier than a man with 19 million.

302.28

A customer asked his banker if the former were worried that he might default on his loan.

"Yes I'm a little worried."

"Good," he replied, "that's what I'm paying 6 percent for."

302.29

A man received a letter appealing for funds. It was addressed to "Occupant." He sat right down and wrote out a check for $1,000 and mailed it back in the postpaid envelope which was enclosed.

The fund raisers were delighted to open the envelope and find the check for $1,000 until they noticed the signature, "Occupant."

302.30

Store owner: "I can't extend any more credit. Your bill right now is bigger than it should be."

Customer: "I know. Make it what it should be and I'll pay it."

302.31

Thrift is a wonderful thing—and who hasn't wished his grandparents had practiced more of it!

302.32

The business tycoon met a friend on a street corner and they started talking. "Say," commented the friend, "I understand your son is in college now. How is he making it?"

"He's not," was the tycoon's reply.

"Oh?" was the friend's questioning comment.

"Nope. I'm making it and he's *spending* it."

302.33

A famous singer was asked about her fortunes during the various stages of her career. She answered, "I've been rich and I've been poor. Either one's all right as long as I have money."

302.34

A girl who says she'll go through anything for a man usually has his bank account in mind.

302.35

"How did Bert manage to spend his rich aunt's bequest so fast?"

"Well, he spent a lot of it on wine, women, and song. He squandered the rest of it."

302.36

"I will answer any two questions for $50," said the gypsy.

"Isn't the price rather high?" remarked the tourist.

"You bet," said the gypsy. "What's your second question?"

302.37

One woman bought an evening gown for a ridiculous price, and her husband thought she got it for an absurd figure.

302.38

If it's such a small world, then why does it cost so much to run it?

302.39

A wife, in a somber moment, said to her husband, "Eternity is much too vast for man to comprehend."

The husband replied, "Take a look at the mortgage."

302.40

"How can I ever let you know what this has meant to me?" asked a middle-aged tourist of her Florentine guide.

"Madame," he replied, "since coinage was invented by the Phoenicians, there has been only one acceptable answer to that question."

302.41

A bank president was extremely self-conscious about his baldness, and wore his hat almost all of the time, indoors and out. One day the porter, a long-time employee, was sweeping out his office. The president said, "Ed, you've been with us for many years now. Why is it," he asked, kidding, "that you've never opened an account with us?"

Ed said, "Well, boss, it's because you always look like you're about to go somewhere."

302.42

A slick saleslady who talked a woman into buying a mink coat asked her, "How would your husband like to be billed, madam. In a series of piddling amounts or in one staggering sum?"

302.43

Couple applying for extension of son's college loan: "We had his board and tuition figured out right, but we didn't count on bail."

302.44

My parents always told me that I couldn't buy happiness— but they didn't say I couldn't rent it.

302.45

The sales representative was concluding his sales talk for a 44-volume encyclopedia.

"Yes, ma'am," he said, "You just put down a tiny deposit, then you don't pay another thing for six months."

"Say," the housewife asked him suspiciously, "who's been telling you about us?"

302.46

An Indian was trying to get a loan for $200, and was asked what security he had to offer.

"Two hundred horses."

This seemed adequate, and he was granted the loan.

When the note came due, he peeled two 100-dollar bills from a roll that would have choked one of those horses, and paid the banker.

The banker, his eyes dancing with the vision of dollar bills, asked the Indian why he didn't leave some of his money in the bank.

Looking the banker straight in the eye, he asked, "How many horses you got?"

302.47

Maid: "Madam, the installment man is here again."

Mistress: "Tell him to take a chair."

302.48

If the price of milk goes any higher, I'll buy a cow and take things into my own hands.

302.49

"What's wrong, Charlie? You look depressed."

"Well, I am. When I left home this morning I had a hundred dollars in this suit. I've looked through every pocket except one, and I can't find it!"

"Why don't you look in that pocket?"

"I'm afraid to. If it isn't there, then I'll really worry."

302.50

My boy came up to me and asked if there was any work he could do to replenish his bank. I told him I couldn't think of anything. So he said, "O.K., how about putting me on welfare?"

302.51

Funny how a dollar can look so big when you take it to church, and so small when you take it to the store.

302.52

Chiseler: A Stone Age accountant.

302.53

A man returning from embassy duty in Japan said he liked the massage baths so much that he had to leave. Asked why his liking the baths made him depart, he replied, "My water bill was three million yen."

302.54

A man bolted from a hotel without paying his tab. The hotel immediately sent him a note which said, "Please send us the amount of your bill."

A week later they received this note in reply, "The amount of my bill was $165.37. Regards."

302.55

"My wife explored my suit pockets last night."

"She find anything?"

"Same as any explorer—enough material for a lecture."

302.56

I was born at the age of two, and spent the next 12 years in the hospital . . . Dad couldn't pay the bill.

302.57

What constitutes a living wage depends upon whether you are giving it or getting it.

302.58

A friend of mine lost a bundle when the stock market skidded, and now he won't even read a book with margins in it.

302.59

"Can I have $35 to buy a new hat?" asked the office manager's wife.

"I should say not," was the grouchy reply. "Do you think money grows on trees? Don't you know I'm not made of money?" The husband launched into a long tirade about economy and the budget.

The wife listened patiently and then said, "Could I at least have $10 to tide me over until you're in a better mood?"

302.60

The playboy walked into a fancy jewelry store late Friday afternoon and charged a $10,000 necklace. On Monday morning he received a frantic call from the store.

"We're going to take the necklace back," said the manager, "Your credit is lousy."

"I know," answered the rake. "And thanks for a fantastic weekend."

302.61

Appearances are deceiving. A 10 dollar bill looks the same as it did 10 years ago.

302.62

Economics—Highbrow talk for "What happened to the money in the cookie jar?"

302.63

Store owner: "Look, you've had this tab for over a year. Tell you what I'll do. I'll forget half of it."
Customer: "Great! I'll forget the other half."

302.64

Accounting—An intricate system of black numbers explaining how the company came out in the red.

302.65

I went in for a loan the other day and found out my credit was so bad they wouldn't even accept my cash.

302.66

When government spends more than it gets, and when labor gets more than it gives, that empty feeling in your pocket is inflation.

302.67

Inflation is being broke with a lot of money in the bank.

302.68

Gold digger—A girl who's got what it takes to take what you've got.

302.69

Census taker: "Does your wife have an independent source of income?"
Husband: "Yeah. Me."

302.70

"Is a penny worth anything these days?"
  "Only at church."

302.71

Money is like fertilizer: It's no good until you spread it around.

302.72

If money could talk, it would ask, "What happened?"

302.73

A nickel goes a long ways, these days, you can carry it around for weeks before you can find something to buy with it.

302.74

Comedian Bill Cosby said he can never figure out foreign currency exchange. So when he gets to a foreign country, he pulls out some greenbacks and says, "Don't hurt me."

302.75
These days they carry you into a hospital fee first.

302.76
When I was young, I used to think that money was the most important thing in life; now that I am older, I know it is.

302.77
Money won't bring you friends. But it gets you a nicer class of enemies.

302.78
Extravagance: the way other people spend money.

302.79
It's better to give than to lend, and it costs about the same.

302.80
Budget—mathematical confirmation of your suspicions.

302.81
Debt: Something you're hardly ever out of.

302.82
A genius is somebody who can do everything except earn a living.

302.83
I really can't complain. My wife has only one extravagance. The checking account.

FOOD
EATING

312.15

Hear about the guy who swallowed a bottle of liquid stockings? Now he needs a garter to hold his stomach up.

312.16

According to the lecturing food-faddist, most of what we eat should have killed us long ago. Meat was murderous; vegetables, vicious; and the water we drank poisonous. Finally, he pointed an accusing finger at a bored and hungry man in the audience. "You, sir," he demanded, "can you tell me what it is that most of us eat at one time or other that's the worst thing in the world for us?"

Without hesitation, the man answered, "Wedding cake!"

312.17

"Wake up, dear! There's a burglar in the kitchen and he's eating the rest of the meat loaf I made tonight."

"Go back to bed. I'll bury him in the morning."

312.18

Bride: "The two things I cook best are meat loaf and apple dumplings."

Groom: "Which is this?"

312.19

The easiest way to clean out the refrigerator is to leave several teen-age boys all alone in the kitchen.

312.20

Raisin: A grape which has wrinkles from lots of worrying.

312.21

An old British colonel returned from the campaigns in India, and was feted at a dinner party. The old gent was seated next to a lovely woman when dinner was served. The lady was amazed to see the fellow pick up each stalk of asparagus, dip it in butter, then wipe it across his brow before putting it in his mouth. Finally, she couldn't stand it anymore, and asked, "Why do you wipe each stalk of asparagus across your brow before putting it in your mouth?"

The colonel replied: "Asparagus! I thought it was broccoli!"

312.22

Two society leaders in an African cannibal tribe were discussing their respective marital troubles. "I don't know what to make of my husband these days," said one.

"Oh, don't let that bother you," said the other. "I have the most delicious recipe I'll send you."

312.23

Husband: "Where does all the money go that I give you for groceries?"
Wife: "Stand sideways and look in the mirror."

312.24

Affluent man (to panhandler): "Why don't you just go down to the mission and get a meal?"
Mendicant: "Gee, don't you ever feel like eating out?"

312.25

A captain who received a complaint about the food barked angrily, "Why, if Napoleon had had that food in Russia, he wouldn't have complained."

"Yes, sir," said the lieutenant, "but it was fresh then."

312.26

I went into a restaurant the other day and had a typical American snack: pizza, chow mein, and blintzes.

312.27

A cannibal chief asked his captive what his line of business had been. The soon-to-be-eaten man replied that he had been assistant editor of a newspaper.

"Cheer up," the chief replied, "you'll soon be editor-in-chief."

312.28

Actually, I wouldn't always be asking the general manager for a raise, but somehow my children found out that other families eat three times a day.

312.29

"Don't eat so much," said the father to his spitting image, "you'll make a pig of yourself. Do you know what a pig is?"

"Yes, Daddy," replied the son. "It's a hog's little boy."

312.30

Everything is artificial these days. A little old lady I know went into a restaurant and started stealing those little packets of saccharin they have for coffee. She stole a hundred of them. Two months later she came down with artificial diabetes.

312.31

A butcher shop in London put up a sign which read, "We make sausage for Queen Elizabeth II." A rival shop across the street immediately put up a sign which proclaimed, "God save the Queen."

312.32

Ya know . . . yesterday I swallowed a doorknob, and no matter what I do, it still turns my stomach.

312.33

We kept a turkey in the refrigerator so long that, when I opened the door, the turkey said, "I don't mind the cold, but every time the light goes out, I step in the jello."

312.34

A friend of mine went into one of those restaurants that has everything on the menu, you know. So he ordered a whale sandwich. They bring him his sandwich, he tastes it, and says, "Hey, just a minute. This isn't whale, it's hippopotamus."

The waiter says, "I know, but we didn't want to cut up a new whale just for one sandwich."

312.35

Newlywed wife: "What will I get if I cook like that every day for a year?"
Husband: "My life insurance."

312.36

The difference between a poor man and a rich man is that one worries over his next meal and the other over his last.

312.37

Husband: "Where am I when you serve the meals from which I always get the leftovers?"

312.38

A cannibal is a guy who loves his fellow man . . . with gravy.

312.39

"Doesn't my cooking just melt in your mouth?" the young bride asked her husband.

"Yes," he answered, "it does. Maybe you could try thawing it out a little more?"

312.40

A hamburger by any other name is considerably more expensive.

312.41

"Do you want these eggs turned over?"

"Yeah. To the Museum of Natural History."

312.42

Diner to waiter: "Did you say this ham was cured?"
Waiter: "Yes."
Diner: "Well, then it's had a relapse."

312.43

Home-cooked meals are great for men—if they're willing to learn how to cook them.

312.44

A codfish lays 10,000 eggs in one day and never says a word. A hen lays one egg and cackles. Ever hear of anybody eating codfish eggs?

312.45

"My wife really loves me—she treats me like a god. She puts a burnt offering before me every night around six."

312.46

My wife is a light eater—when it becomes light, she starts eating.

312.47

My wife cooks such a lousy breakfast that my daughter calls it morning sickness.

312.48

"And how did you find your steak, sir?"
   "I just moved a potato, and there it was."

312.49

"I'll take the two-dollar dinner."
   "On white, rye, or whole wheat?"

312.50

A workman opened his lunchbox and moaned, "Oh no! Peanut butter! Always this rotten crummy peanut butter!"
   "Well, if you don't like peanut butter," said a friend, "why not have your wife make you a different kind of sandwich?"
   "You leave my wife out of this," said the worker, "I always make my own sandwiches."

FRIENDS
FRIENDSHIP

320.50

One thing about me ... my friends either dislike me or they hate me.

320.51

If you make just one new friend every day, at the end of a year you'll be stuck with 364 new friends.

320.52

Some guests for a weekend, I look on with sorrow: Here today and here tomorrow.

320.53

Show me a friend in need, and I'll show you a pain in the neck.

320.54

Be nice to your friends and acquaintances. If it weren't for them, you'd be a total stranger.

GAMES
GAMBLING

328.20

A guy put a bet on a horse once, and his friend, a bookie, took him to task over it. "That nag isn't good enough for the glue factory. He may die at the gate. I'll give you a million to one on him." The man took the bet for a dollar.

The horse came in by a head, and the bookie paid off. As he was counting out the cash, the bookie said, "You must feel pretty good about this one."

"Not so hot," the man grumbled. "I've been betting the ponies all my life. I finally hit a million-to-one shot, and all I've got on him is a lousy buck."

328.21

A Broadway disc jockey walked dejectedly into the station, and the station manager asked him where he had been.

"A poor people's march," was his only reply.

"Well, that's good. I don't see why you're so down. Where was it?"

"On the way back from Roosevelt Raceway," he answered.

328.22

An Arizona sheriff closed down a bunch of slot machines on the authority of a law which said that steel traps could not be used to catch dumb animals.

328.23

A novice bridge player was set two on a contract that he should have made. He turned to the best player in the foursome and said, "How would you have played that last hand?"

The man replied, "Under an assumed name."

328.24

(Before leaving) ... My wife (girl) is having friends over this evening for canasta, and I've got to hurry home and mark the cards.

328.25

A man came up to a card table where the indefatigable W. C. Fields was playing poker.

"Is this a game of chance?" he asked.

"Not the way I play it," Fields replied.

328.26

I was at a family picnic last Fourth of July, and we all wanted to play horseshoes. But my mother-in-law refused to go barefoot.

328.27

A friend of mine went to the track, made a "mental bet" and lost his mind.

328.28

Haggerty had a miserable run of luck at the track and was down to his last 10-spot when he happened to glimpse his parish priest just as he made a gesture before a horse in the paddock. "With the holy father blessin' the creature," reasoned Haggerty, "how kin he lose?" So he put the whole 10 right on the nose to win.

There were eight horses in the race—and Haggerty's choice finished eighth. A few days later he encountered the priest on the street and grumbled, "It's let down I feel, that's what! I bet on a horse because ye stop to bless it, and begorra, it finished last!"

"You should have watched more closely," the priest told him, "I wasn't blessing that horse, I was giving him the last rites."

328.29

I just love to sit in the parlor with my girl, and turn out all the lights . . . I've got checkers that glow in the dark.

328.30

"Now don't lie, Johnny. Did Daddy really take you to the zoo?"

"He sure did. And one of the animals paid 30 to 1."

328.31

A judge asked a locksmith what he was doing in a gambling joint when it was raided by the police. The man answered, "I was making a bolt for the door."

328.32

Do you know how to come back from Las Vegas with a small fortune? Go with a large fortune.

328.33

Racetrack—The only place where windows clean people.

328.34

The four card players were going crazy from the incessant chatter of a kibitzer and when the pest left the room for a moment, one suggested: "When he comes back let's make up a game nobody's heard of. Maybe that'll shut him up."

When the kibitzer returned, the dealer dealt 13 cards apiece. He looked at his hand and said, "I have a forstant, so I bet 50 cents."

The second man said, "I have a sniffle and I raise you a buck."

The third man said, "I've got a bloomquist and I'll raise you a dollar."

"Are you crazy?" shouted the kibitzer. "You're never gonna beat a sniffle with a lousy bloomquist!"

328.35

A lawyer fell madly in love with his partner's wife. He tried to be casual about it, but it finally became too much. He went to his partner and told him everything.

The partner was quite understanding, but said, "This situation cannot be allowed to continue. Tell you what I'll do; I'll play you one game of gin, winner takes the woman home."

"Great," said the other, "and why don't we play for a penny a point just to make it interesting?"

328.36

A renowned gambler died, and his funeral was packed with his professional friends. In the eulogy, the preacher said: "Lefty is not dead, he only sleeps."

From the back of the church came, "I got a C-note says he's dead."

328.37

"I hear your boss made a killing in Las Vegas."

"I suppose you could say that. He went there in a $9,000 Mercedes and came back in an $80,000 Greyhound bus."

328.38

Overheard at the track: "I don't have a cent to bet today. My wife blew the whole bankroll on the rent."

328.39

In Las Vegas, the odds are you won't get even.

328.40

I know a girl who can't stand going to the races. She'd much rather stay home and curl up with a good bookie.

328.41

I believe you can tell the future from a deck of cards . . . I once looked through a deck and found six aces . . . right away I knew someone was going to the hospital.

328.42

A horse player was talking about an unfortunate wager he had just lost, and said, "It would have been a photo finish but, by the time my horse finished, it was too dark to take a picture."

328.43

"Why is it," said a man, "that Frank is lucky at cards and is completely unlucky with horses?"

"Easy. They don't let him shuffle the horses."

328.44

First salesman: "So you taught your wife to play poker?"
Second salesman: "Sure, and it was a great idea. Last night, I won back almost half of my salary."

328.45

A husband who was an ardent bowler played in a league every Wednesday, come hell or high water. One Wednesday, however, he didn't come home. Three years passed before he finally showed up again and his devoted wife was more than overjoyed to see him.

"I must call all our friends," she said through tears of joy.

"What for?" her husband asked.

"Because they'll all be so happy to know you've returned. We'll have a homecoming party this evening."

"What," the husband said with disbelief, "on bowling night?"

328.46

Playing cards can be a dangerous experience—but then so can any game in which you hold hands.

328.47

Thoroughbred: The only animal that can take hundreds of people for a ride at the same time.

GIFTS

338.50

A producer gave a starlet a string of pearls for her birthday. A friend chided him, and asked why he didn't give something practical, like a car.

The producer replied, "Did you ever hear of a phony car?"

338.51

A husband came home and announced that he bought a plot in an exclusive cemetery for an anniversary present. His wife knew her way around, and told him she thought it was a great idea. The next year, however, he came home empty-handed and she quietly inquired if another present were forthcoming.

"Come on," he replied, "you haven't even used the one I bought you last year."

338.52

A friend of mine said his teen-agers gave him a nice surprise for his birthday. They let him drive the car for the whole weekend.

338.53

The enterprising office boy canvassed all the men in the office about two weeks before Christmas. To each one he put the question: "What size collar do you wear?"

Of course, this veiled hint of a forthcoming gift brought him stacks of valuable loot from his co-workers who ordinarily wouldn't even have thought of sending him a card. In return, however, each donor received a card from the office boy. It read:

"To Jack, the greatest guy who ever put his head in a size 15½ collar."

338.54

Betty: "I believe my husband is the most generous man in the world."

"How's that?" Jane asked Betty.

Betty: "Well, I gave him a dozen of the loveliest neckties for Christmas, and he took them right down and gave them to the Salvation Army."

338.55

A boy walked into the lingerie department of a store and shyly told the saleslady he wanted a slip for a present for his mother.

"It would help if I knew if she is tall or short, stout or thin," the girl told him.

"She's just perfect," the boy replied. The saleslady wrapped up a size 34. A few days later the mother arrived at the department to exchange it for a size 52.

338.56

My mother-in-law sent me two sweaters for Christmas, so when she arrived for a visit, I was wearing one of them.

She immediately glared at me and asked: "What's the matter, didn't you like the other one?"

338.57

The sales manager's wedding anniversary was just a few days off and he was in a quandary about what to get as a present for his wife. In desperation, he asked his secretary what she thought might be appropriate.

The secretary suggested various apparel items, jewelry, an automobile, etc., but none of the items met with the manager's approval. "Well, if you can't find anything else," she said, "why don't you just give her money?"

"Money!" shouted the sales manager. "I can't give her money! You have to pay list price for that!"

GOSSIP

346.50

"I've heard a great deal about you, Senator," the Washington hostess gushed.

"Possibly," the politician said, "but you can't prove a thing."

346.51

Town gossip: Prattlesnake.

346.52

Mrs. Alice Roosevelt Longworth, long a treasured part of the Washington social scene, says: If you don't have anything nice to say about a person, lean closer.

346.53

A manager of a small company would leave the office every day precisely at 3:00 p.m., and return a half-hour later. He was so consistent about this that the office gossips became curious about where he went. Finally, after months had passed, the president of the firm got wind of the exodus and, being curious, too, asked about it.

The manager replied: "Every day I get into my car, drive down to the railroad tracks and wait. Then, at 3:12, when the eastbound freight goes by, I sigh and say to myself, 'Thank heaven, there goes something I don't have to push!' "

HABITS

358.50

A women walked up to a boy she caught smoking and said, "Young man, does your mother know you are smoking?"

The boy countered: "Lady, does your husband know you are stopping strange men on the street?"

358.51

A man was trying to quit smoking, so a friend advised, "Why not do what my late friend Harry did. He walked around day and night with a toothpick in his mouth until he broke the habit."

"That sounds great," said the other, "but you said your 'late' friend. What did he die of?"

"Dutch elm disease."

358.52

There is no rainbow at the end of pot.

358.53

A friend of mine has read so much about the harmful effects of smoking that he has decided to give up reading.

358.54

The injured man went to his doctor and asked him to look at his ailing knee. After a careful examination the doctor asked, "How long have you had this condition?"

"Two weeks," the patient said.

"My goodness!" the doctor exclaimed. "Your knee is severely fractured and you've waited two weeks to come to me? Why on earth did you wait this long?"

"Because, Doc, every time I say there's something wrong with me my wife insists I stop smoking."

358.55
Tobacco: A nauseating weed consumed by only two creatures: man and large green worms. The worm doesn't know any better.

366.30

A man partook generously of food and drink one New Year's Eve, and subsequently developed a severe intestinal cramp. He went to the doctor and asked, "Do you think the trouble is with my appendix?"

"No," said the doctor, "I think it's with your table of contents."

366.31

A man was near death, and his wife asked what he would like to eat. He said he smelled stew cooking in the kitchen, and said "I'd like a little of that, it smells so good."

"Oh, no, you don't," said the wife, "I'm saving that for the wake."

366.32

Sam: "I used to think I was a beagle. But the psychiatrist cured me."
Bruce: "How are you now?"
Sam: "Great. Feel my nose."

366.33

"Now I know why I got a bad back. We got some ultramodern furniture in the office and I found out I've been sitting in the waste basket."

366.34

Doctor: "You have acute indigestion."
Girl: "Now listen here, I came here to be examined, not complimented."

366.35

"How do you decide when a patient is well enough to leave?" asked a visitor in an insane asylum.

"Well," explained the attendant, "the doctors are too overworked to keep close check on all the patients, so we turn on the faucet that supplies the big trough over there. We leave the water running and tell the patients to take buckets and empty all the water out of the trough."

"How does that show anything?" asked the visitor.

"Well, a patient who is cured will turn off the faucet."

"Well, I declare," marveled the visitor. "I never would have thought of that."

366.36

My agent gets 10 percent of everything I have, except the migraine headaches and indigestion.

366.37

Nothing is quite as sad as a reporter in a bar with an unlimited expense account and ulcers.

366.38

Epitaph on the tombstone of a hypochondriac: "See, I told ya I was sick."

366.39

Perhaps the best advice on health ever given was by ageless baseball wonder Satchel Paige, who said: "Avoid fried meats which anger up the blood. If your stomach disputes you, lie down, and pacify it with cool thoughts. Keep the juices flowing by jangling around gently as you move. Go very light on the vices—such as carrying on in society. The social ramble ain't restful. Avoid running at all times. And, finally, don't look back. Something may be gaining on you."

366.40

President Nixon's medical bill is designed to cover "catastrophic illness." At today's prices, that could be a hangnail!

366.41

"I simply don't know what to do, Doctor," complained the upset wife. "My husband thinks he's Moses."

The doctor urged her to try understanding in a case such as this and that in time the poor fellow's obsession with his own greatness would pass.

"Gee," said the worried lady. "I hope it's soon. I'm getting sick and tired of him parting the waters every time I take a bath."

366.42

Said one woman to a friend, "My husband passed away last month. He had a stroke."

"Really," said her friend, "was it serious?"

366.43

Old Paddy was near death's door, and his friends came over to visit him. He was feeling low, so the boys decided to cheer him up.

They climbed up to his small attic room, and Mike said, "Will ya be going with us to the boat races this weekend? Ya look fit to row yourself."

They noticed his spirits pick up immediately, so Dan said, "Paddy, me boy, you'll be back on the job so soon you'll be wishing you were back here resting."

And Tom added, "You never looked better in your life, and you'll be looking even better tomorrow."

Paddy's spirits soared, and he felt better. They visited for a little while longer, then the boys started to leave. But Mike nearly hit his head on the door frame. He stopped, felt the width of the frame, then said, "They'll never get a coffin out o' here."

366.44

Doctor: "Well, you will get along all right, Mr. Jones. Your left leg is swollen, but I wouldn't worry about it."

Mr. Jones: "No? And if your leg was swollen, I wouldn't worry about it either."

366.45

Patient: "Nurse, why are all the shades down?"

Nurse: "There was a fire across the street and we didn't want you to wake up and think the operation was a failure."

366.46

A fanatical faith healer ran into an old friend and asked how things were.

"Not so good," complained the friend. "My wife is ill."

"Your wife is not sick," contradicted the fanatic. "She only *thinks* she is sick. Have faith and remember this."

A few weeks later they met again and the faith healer asked, "How's your wife now, my friend?"

"Worse," groaned the friend. "She thinks she's dead."

366.47

A man was driving by an insane asylum when he had a flat tire. He pulled over to the side of the road and began to change it. He took the flat tire off and was in the act of replacing it with the spare when he accidentally knocked all the lug nuts off the car. They all rolled down a nearby sewer.

He was absolutely flabbergasted, didn't have any idea what to do, when one of the inmates who happened to be walking by stopped and suggested that he take one lug off each of the other tires, put the spare on with three lugs, and drive to a service station to get more of them.

"Gee," said the man, "that's a great idea. I never would have thought of it. But . . . you know, how did you happen to think of it . . . I mean . . ."

"Oh, that's all right," said the inmate, "I may be crazy, but I'm not stupid."

HOLIDAYS

378.50
Student: "Do the Mexicans have a Fourth of July?"
Teacher: "Of course not."
Student: "Do they go right from the third to the fifth?"

378.51
Christmas is a time when you get homesick—even when you're home.

378.52
This year all the holidays are being switched around except one—April Fool's Day. That'll still be on April 15.

378.53
I used to be an atheist but had to give it up—not enough holidays.

HOTELS

384.50

A hotel manager received this letter from a salesman: "Have you suitable accommodations where I can put up with my wife?"

384.51

"What's this big item on your expense account?"
   "That's my hotel bill."
   "Well, don't buy any more hotels."

384.52

I was in a hotel in Miami recently that was so big that by the time I got to my room, I owed two days' rent.

384.53

Salesman Sam registered at a small-town hotel and then went into the dining room for dinner.

The waitress began a long spiel about the virtues of the hotel's famed potato soup and, finally, after a long argument, Sam convinced her that he hated potato soup and would have none under any circumstances.

Later that night, the man in the room next to Sam suffered severe stomach pains and his wife telephoned a local doctor and asked him to come quick. The wife met the doctor in the lobby and told him that only an enema would help her husband but that he undoubtedly would make an awful fuss about it.

Unwittingly, the physician went into the wrong room and applied the treatment to Sam.

Several weeks later a friend remarked he was going through the same town and asked Sam about the hotel.

"A wonderful place," said Sam. "But when they offer you potato soup, *take it with the dinner!*"

384.54

An executive in charge of the convention called the hotel's engineer to complain about the temperature in the meeting room. The engineer tried to dismiss the complaint as a very temporary condition and finally asked, "Is it really that cold in there?"

"Cold!" shouted the harried meeting planner. "Why it's so cold, every time we close the door the light goes out!"

384.55

"What was the name of that hotel we stayed at in Cleveland?"

"Ah, come on. Think of it. I don't want to have to dig through the towels again."

HOUSE
HOUSING   HOUSEWIFE   HOUSEKEEPING

386.50
Stucco—What a lot of house hunters are getting these days.

386.51
There is a man who carries so many mortgages on his home that he refers to it as his "lien-to."

386.52
A prospective buyer, looking at a house near a river bank, asked the realtor if water got into the cellar. "This cellar is as dry as the Sahara," the realtor told him.

A month later the buyer went back to the realtor. "You know that house you sold me with the Sahara cellar? I put two mousetraps down there and so far I've caught a catfish and a bass."

386.53
If you have no apartment, you're a vagrant. If you have two, you're a swinger.

386.54
The king of a tribe on a south sea island, after many years, found that his throne was wearing out. It was fixed constantly, but to no avail, and finally had to be replaced. A new throne was installed, but the king, for sentimental reasons, had the old one stored in his hut by having it tied to the ceiling. One night during a typhoon, it blew down and clunked the king on the head.

The moral is that people who live in grass houses shouldn't stow thrones.

386.55

The stuffy matron was explaining to the unsympathetic painter what color she wanted her drawing room done in. "I want a sort of yellowy purple that is a cross between bluey pink and greeny green."

The painter replied, "Look, lady, no such color exists. It's just a pigment of your imagination."

386.56

Tenant: "This building is repulsive. Last night two rats were fighting in my room."

Landlord: "Well, waddya want for 10 bucks a week—a bullfight?"

386.57

For years there's been talk of a housing shortage . . . don't you believe it. It's just a vicious rumor started by a bunch of people with no place to live.

386.58

Watch out before you move into an open-housing area. A friend of mine moved into one recently and found that he had no walls.

386.59

Early American furniture: A black-and-white TV set.

386.60

A beautiful Hungarian blonde was being shown through a penthouse apartment. The owner pointed to a section of the suite and said, "Over here we have the master bedroom, bath and den."

"And den what?" the blonde demanded.

386.61

Tenant: "This darn roof is leaking on our heads. How long
is this going to continue?"
Landlord: "Whaddaya think I am, a weatherman?"

386.62

Eddie Cantor used to tell this one: A housewife complained, "I don't like this apartment, Joe. There are no
curtains in the bathroom and every time I take a bath, the
neighbors can see me."

"That's all right, Rachel," the husband soothed. "When
the neighbors see you, they'll buy the curtains."

HUMAN RELATIONS

390.40
A unilateral agreement? You can only make it with yourself, because if anyone else is around, they won't allow it.

390.41
There are people who make things happen, people who watch things happen, and people who don't know what happened.

390.42
Before trying to keep up with the Joneses, find out where they're going.

390.43
Some people strengthen the society just by being the kind of people they are.

390.44
A committee is a group of the unfit, appointed by the unwilling, to do the unnecessary.

390.45
The two sides of every argument are often what give it no end.

390.46
A Texan who ran an American oil company in North Africa said to a group of incoming engineers: "Our job here is to promote good neighborliness. So if they say Africa is bigger than Texas, agree with them."

HUMOR

394.50
Sense of humor: What makes you laugh at something that would make you mad if it had happened to you.

394.51
A man once told a joke at a dinner, and no one laughed. He quickly added: "The interesting thing about that story is that stupid people never get the point of it." Everyone laughed.

394.52
When the Lord handed out humor, woman was late, as usual. She arrived just in time to get the last laugh.

IDENTITY
IDENTIFY

402.50

Toots Shor once boarded a cab and said, "Take me to the best restaurant in New York."

Without a word, the cabbie took him to his own eatery. Highly complimented, Shor gave the driver a 10-dollar bill. The driver said, "Gee, thanks, Mr. Shor."

402.51

Too great a sense of identity makes a man feel he can do no wrong. And too little does the same.

402.52

Psychiatrist: "Congratulations, you're cured."
Patient: "Thanks for nothing. Before I came to you I was Teddy Roosevelt. Now I'm a nobody."

402.53

My sister-in-law thought she heard her son coming in the back door, so she yelled from the living room, "I'm in here, dear."

A voice came from the kitchen and said, "Gee, lady, I ain't your regular milkman."

402.54

The trouble with today's individualists is that they are getting harder and harder to tell apart.

402.55

When you hear the word "inevitable," watch out! An enemy of humanity has identified himself.

INSURANCE

416.50

We watched Ben Hur on television, and wasn't that a great chariot race? Charlton Heston cut off the driver on his right, sideswiped the one on his left, rammed the one up ahead. Then came that wonderful scene where they canceled his insurance!

416.51

When an insurance investigator returned from a recent fire, his boss asked what had caused the blaze.

"Friction," the investigator said angrily.

"Two things rubbing together, eh?"

"Yeah," the adjuster said, "the fire was caused by rubbing a $10,000 insurance policy against a $7,000 house."

416.52

Two vacationing businessmen were comparing notes on the beach at Waikiki. One said to the other, "I got $100,000 for flood damage."

"Tell me," said the other, "how do you set a flood?"

416.53

A would-be client demanded to know why an insurance agent had failed to send him a policy.

"Remember when you were taking the physical?" asked the agent, "and the doctor punched holes in that card?"

"Sure," said the man. "That was for a computer."

"No, it was actually for the doctor's player piano. He puts it in the piano and the tune it plays tells us whether to sell a policy."

"You're kidding," said the customer, "what did mine play?"

"Nearer my God to Thee."

416.54

My brother-in-law is a notorious skinflint. We got off the plane the other day and he said, "Well, here goes $2.50 worth of insurance down the drain."

416.55

Farmer Thomas' barn had just gone up in smoke, and his insurance agent was trying to explain that he couldn't collect cash for it. "Read the policy," he insisted. "All our company agrees to do is build you another barn exactly like the one that's been destroyed."

Farmer Thomas, apoplectic with rage, thundered, "If that's the way you varmints do business, cancel the policy on my wife before it's too late."

416.56

The grieving widow's husband had been hit by a bus, and the company—clearly at fault—lost no time in seeing to it that the lady was properly compensated for her loss. When the bus company's agent arrived, the widow was in tears. He promptly presented her with a check for $50,000. Through her tears, the widow looked at the check and said sadly, "Thank you, sir, thank you. I'd willingly return $3,000 of this to have my husband back again today."

416.57

Arson—Fire caused by the friction between the mortgage and the insurance policy.

416.58

The sale was wrapped up, and the salesman was just putting the finishing touches on the policy. "Let's see, you want monthly payments on a straight life, right?"

"Well," said the customer. "I'd like to mess around a little on Saturday nights."

INTELLIGENCE

420.50

A woman said to her husband, "I can't decide whether to go to a palmist or a mind reader."

The husband replied, "Go to a palmist—at least he'll have something to work with."

420.51

An intellectual but dizzy poetess was bugging a professor one day. He eventually turned to her and said, "You may have an I.Q. of 150, but you're missing the first 90 points."

420.52

Genius: A fellow who aims at something nobody else can see and hits it.

420.53

They say that human intelligence is several million years old, but it sure doesn't seem to act its age.

420.54

An intelligent minority never seems to stay that way after it becomes a majority.

420.55

A young mother was telling her son about his grandfather— a man so strong that at the age of 75 he would still swim the river in front of his house three times every morning before breakfast.

"Don't you think your grandpop was really quite a guy?" she asked.

"It doesn't seem to me he was real smart," he said. "I would have made a fourth time and ended up where my clothes were."

JOBS

430.30

The applicant for a sales job stood before the sales manager. "Your references, please."

The lad smiled. "I didn't bring any. Like my picture, they don't do me justice."

430.31

When Dudley, the slow-moving clerk in a small store, was not around one morning, a customer asked, "Where's Dudley? Is he sick?"

"He isn't here any more," came the reply.

"That so?" said the customer. "Got anybody in mind for the vacancy?"

The response was terse: "Dudley didn't leave a vacancy."

430.32

Comment on the War on Poverty: Today millions are idle—but, thank goodness, most of them have jobs.

430.33

A wealthy landowner in England advertised for a chauffeur. From the letters of application he selected the three most promising men. When they arrived for the interview, he took them to the top of a cliff near his home. He asked each how close he could drive to the precipice.

The first man boasted that he could drive within a few inches.

The second man more modestly estimated that he could drive within a couple of feet.

The third man, unnerved by the whole idea, gulped and said he wouldn't care to drive within a mile of the place.

He got the job.

430.34

Two friends who hadn't seen each other for some time met on the street. The first one said, "Hi, Frank, what are you doing? I heard you applied for a government job."

"Nothing. I got it."

430.35

Father: "Son, what would you like to do when you grow up?"

Son: "I'd like to drive a Sherman tank."

Father: "Well, son, I'm not going to stand in your way."

430.36

If your job is dull and your pay is low and you don't get enough recognition, friends . . . QUIT. So what's to lose?

430.37

"Yes," said the store personnel manager to the man applying for a job in the men's clothing department. "What we're after is a man of vision; a man with drive; a man who can inspire others; a man who can pull our bowling team out of last place."

430.38

Another bright lad got tired of working as an office boy for a law firm and decided to try his luck at selling. He applied for a job and, during the interview, the sales manager was impressed with the youngster's quick intelligence and sincerity. All went well during the interview until the sales manager asked, "How much do you make a week with the law firm?"

"I get $260 a week," was the reply.

"Two hundred and sixty dollars! Per week?"

"Sure," said the lad. "I get $60 in cash and the rest in legal advice."

430.39

In the halcyon days before women's lib, a college professor was counseling a coed about her future plans.

"What are your inclinations?" he inquired.

She replied, "My very soul burns, yearns and pulsates to give the world a life work that shall be brilliant in scope and weirdly entrancing in the vastness of its structural beauty."

He replied, "My dear, you're a born hat maker."

430.40

My brother-in-law had a terrible accident last week—he found a job.

430.41

A night watchman makes a living without doing a day's work.

430.42

Young men object that they can't get a job if their hair is long. They ought to see how tough it is to get one when the hair is sparse and grey.

430.43

Ambition is a great and rewarding feeling. Who can forget the young necrophiliac who, through hard work and dedication, achieved his lifelong ambition and became a mortician.

430.44

Placement counselor to young applicant: "Your test scores indicate that your best opportunities lie in a field where your father has considerable influence."

430.45

Overheard: "Doc, I can't pay my bill. I slowed down just like you told me to—and I lost my job."

430.46

"What we need is a good worrier," said the executive to the job applicant. "A man who can come in every day and just sit around and worry. $300 a week. You want it?"

"Certainly," exclaimed the job hunter. "But tell me: Who pays me the three hundred?"

"Ah, hah!" said the businessman. "That's your first worry!"

430.47

A man was trying to get a job as an apprentice plumber. "Have you got any references?" asked the plumber to whom he was applying.

"I sure do," said the man, "but I left them home; I'll be glad to go and get them."

"Never mind, you'll do," said the plumber.

430.48

Did you hear about the street cleaner who was fired because he couldn't keep his mind in the gutter?

JUSTICE
JUDGES   JURISDICTION

432.40

A prisoner was sitting in his cell when his lawyer walked in.

"Don't worry about a thing," began the lawyer, "my uncle is the judge. I'll prove that you were insane or in Europe, that the witnesses were paid off by the D.A., and that you were really a federal agent in disguise. Meanwhile, try to escape."

432.41

Some of those old proverbial expressions just don't apply in all cases. Like "Early to bed, early to rise, makes a man healthy, wealthy, and wise." Tell that to a guy doing 99 years.

432.42

Judge: "Couldn't this matter have been settled out of court?"

Defendant: "That's just what we were doing, your honor, when the cops busted in."

432.43

Jury: Twelve people chosen to decide who has the better attorney.

432.44

"You told me that if I was nice to the judge he'd let me off."

"Well, were you?"

"Sure. I said, 'Mornin' your Honor, how are you?' and he said, 'Fine—$100'."

432.45

A lawyer called on his imprisoned client and explained why he had postponed the trial for such a long period. "What I'm looking for is a judge who has a real sense of humor."

432.46

The trial had been underway for several days. The defense was about to start its summary of the case when the judge noticed only 11 men were in the jury box. "Where is the other juror?" he asked angrily.

"It's all right, your honor," reasoned the foreman pleasantly. "He was called away on business, but he left his verdict with me."

432.47

"Would you please repeat the exact phrase the defendant used?"

"But it's not fit to tell a gentleman."

"Then lean over and whisper it to the judge."

432.48

Boy, am I mad!! I just got a call from the police. They've got my kid down at the station . . . they just arrested him for stealing an apple from a pushcart . . . and threw him in jail for impersonating a police officer.

432.49

A man was charged with a minor offense.

"Is there anyone here who can vouch for you?" asked the judge.

"Certainly," said the man, "the sheriff."

"But, your honor," said the sheriff, "I don't even know this man."

"See, your honor?" said the defendant. "I've lived in this county for 13 years and the sheriff doesn't even know me."

LABOR

442.50

She was married to him for 40 years, and for 40 years he didn't do a lick of work. Then he died. She had him cremated, took the ashes home and put them in an hourglass. "Now, you worthless bum," she muttered, "at last you're going to work."

442.51

Idleness: A state that can be enjoyed only when there's lots of work to do.

442.52

My brother-in-law claims he is a self-made man. If that is the case, it's the worst example of unskilled labor I've ever seen.

442.53

"The devil finds work for idle hands." Now if we could only get private industry to do the same!

442.54

Abraham Lincoln once took a sack of grain to a mill whose miller was known to be the laziest man in 12 counties. After watching the man for a while, the rail-splitter wearily remarked, "I could eat that grain as fast as you're grinding it."

"Indeed," said the miller, "and just how long do you think you could keep that up?"

"Until I starved to death," answered the future president.

442.55

My kid is no dummy! When he grows up he wants to be the president . . . of a labor union.

442.56

A group of students was watching with close attention as the professor of archeology exhumed the wrapped body of an ancient Egyptian mummy. "Judging from the various utensils buried with him," observed the professor in scholarly tones, "this fellow must have been an Egyptian plumber."

"Wouldn't it be fascinating," said one of the awed onlookers, "if he could be brought back to life?"

"Interesting, but risky," the archeologist observed dryly. "Somebody might have to pay him union scale for the time he has spent in here."

LANGUAGE

448.40
Synonym—A word you use when you can't spell the one you were thinking of.

448.41
If you add just one new word to your vocabulary each day, at the end of a year your friends will wonder just who you think you are.

448.42
Platitude: This is a dull old saw which everyone uses but no one ever takes time to sharpen.

448.43
I know a man with an outstanding vocabulary. He can describe a pretty girl without using his hands.

448.44
They spell it Vinci and pronounce it Vinchy; foreigners always spell better than they pronounce.

448.45
The story goes that, when Captain Cook discovered Australia, his sailors brought a strange animal aboard ship whose name they did not know. Cook sent a sailor ashore to inquire of the natives the name of this creature. He returned and reported it was known as a "kangaroo." Many years passed before it was learned that when the natives were asked the name of the animal and replied, "Kangaroo," they were simply asking, "What did you say?"

448.46

The ladies club was in full swing, and each mother was boasting about the linguistic ability of her children. One said, "My Percy speaks French with a beautiful accent."

Another added, "My Henrietta speaks graceful Spanish."

Not to be outdone, a third mother piped up, "Yeah? Well, my Rodney speaks Esperanto like a native!"

448.47

"Boss," said the longshore foreman to the terminal manager, "the boys are getting kinda hedgy about this new freight loader you brought in yesterday."

"Why so?" asked the boss. "He seemed to check out extremely well."

"Maybe," said the foreman, "but this morning he hit his toe on a crate of ball bearings, so he yells out, "Oh, the wicked perversity of inanimate objects."

448.48

Woman: "Irregardless, I don't need none."

Salesman: "How do you know? I might be selling grammar books."

448.49

Drawing on my fine command of language I said nothing.

448.50

A Boston spinster was shocked at the language used by workmen repairing telephone wires near her home, so she wrote to the telephone company. The manager immediately asked the foreman on the job to make a report, and here's what the foreman said:

"Spike Williams and me were on this job. I was up on the pole and accidentally let some hot lead fall on Spike—and it went down his neck. Then Spike looked up at me and said, 'Really, Harry, you must be more careful'."

LAW
LAWYERS

454.50

"And how is Lawyer Brown doing?"

"Not well at all. In fact, the poor man is lying at death's door."

"That's the old spirit. At death's door and still lying."

454.51

Judge: "Do you have anything to offer this court before sentence is passed on you?"

Defendant: "No, your honor. I had $100, but my lawyer took it."

454.52

A shyster is the other man's lawyer.

454.53

"What is the object of legislation?"

"The greatest good to the greatest number."

"What do you consider the greatest number?"

"Number one."

454.54

A popular Broadway star became involved in politics and decided to back an unpopular candidate for governor. He approached a very prominent and influential retired attorney and asked if he would also campaign for his man.

"I'm sorry, I can't," replied the lawyer. "I've retired from criminal practice."

LIFE
LIVING

464.50

I would rather live in a world where my life
by mystery than live in a world so small th.   mind
could comprehend it.

464.51

Life's unfairness is not irrevocable; we can help balance the
scales for others, if not always for ourselves.

464.52

A rolling stone gathers no moss, but the rolling stone
doesn't care. Momentum is what it wants to gather.

464.53

It is an irony of life that we get bent from hard work and
broke without it.

464.54

If life had a second edition, how would you correct the
proofs?

464.55

Do you realize the value of life? Just think . . . without it,
you're dead!

464.56

You can't just go on being a good egg. You must either
hatch or go bad.

LISTENING

470.50

George Bernard Shaw had been bored nearly to tears by the long and pedantic discourse of a man who was trying to impress him.

"You know," said Shaw to the man, "between the two of us we know all there is to be known."

The man was delighted, and said, "Really? How is that?"

Shaw answered, "You seem to know everything except that you are a bore. And I know that."

470.51

Listen, or thy tongue will keep thee deaf.

470.52

A deaf old gentleman decided that a hearing aid was too expensive, so he got an ordinary piece of wire and wrapped it around his ear.

"Do you hear better now with that wire around your ear?" a friend asked.

"No, but everybody talks louder."

470.53

"My mother talks to herself," one boy said to another.

His friend replied, "So does mine, but she doesn't realize it. She thinks I'm listening."

470.54

When you talk, you only hear what you know. When you listen, you hear what someone else knows.

LITERATURE

472.50

A minor poet once complained to Oscar Wilde that there was a "conspiracy of silence" against his poems in the press. "It is nothing short of a conspiracy, Oscar," the man said. "What do you suggest I do?"

To which Wilde replied, "Join it."

472.51

A scholarly professor of literature had gone slumming to a pool hall. He returned to the university dejected, and a friend asked about his gloom. The scholar replied, "I was missing shots, so someone said, 'Put a little of that old English on it.' So I recited 'Beowulf' and still missed."

472.52

Shakespeare was a famous playwright who made a living writing things for people to quote.

472.53

Shakespeare, like everyone else, had to do a little editing. Like Romeo said to Juliet, "We can't go on like this—I'm getting a stiff neck."

472.54

"How is your study of English literature coming?" the father asked his college freshman son.

"Well, I'm closely following the progression of many great works."

"How do you mean?"

"I'm going from bard to verse."

LOVE
ROMANCE   COURTSHIP

480.25

Hoarsely, the impassioned suitor begged, "Whisper those three words that will make me walk on air."

So she sweetly told him "Go hang yourself."

480.26

I've been parking in Lover's Lane for over a year now . . . and ya know . . . it's more fun if ya take a girl along.

480.27

"Why so glum?" a fellow asked his friend. "New girl throw you over?"

"No," was the answer, "but I'm having doubts about her. She took a new apartment Tuesday and spent all day Wednesday going from telephone booth to telephone booth changing her number on the walls."

480.28

One piece of sound advice about love was passed from father to son. The message was, "Protect your heart as you would your other vital organs."

480.29

Courtship is the moonlight of love—marriage the light bill.

480.30

"Who was that you were out with last night?"

"An archaeologist."

"Where did you dig him up?"

480.31
A good friend forgives your faults; a lover doesn't see any.

480.32
It was the parting of the ways. "We've had good times together, Ben," she admitted, "but what I thought was love for you was only a sisterly affection. Since I met Morris I've known that he is the man for me. Here is your engagement ring."

"Do you know where Morris is now?" he asked sadly.

"Why?" she asked, considerably alarmed. "You're not going to hurt him are you?"

"No, I'll leave that to you. All I want to do is see if I can sell him this engagement ring."

480.33
What we call Lover's Lane ... the Eskimos call Blubber's Lane ... I guess that's 'cause they have a whale of a time.

480.34
If at first you don't succeed, you can always call up some other girl.

480.35
A friend of mine's sister has waited so long for her dreamboat to come in that her dock was collapsed.

480.36
Platonic love is like being invited down to the cellar for a drink of root beer.

480.37
A bachelor can be miss-led only so far.

480.38

Scholarly Canadian humorist Stephen Leacock once said, "Many a man in love with a dimple makes the mistake of marrying the whole girl."

480.39

"I'm telling you for the last time that you cannot come in and kiss me!"

"I knew you'd weaken."

480.40

Boy: Meet me at the Ritz-Carlton at eight.
Girl: Say, the Ritz! That's a really nice place.
Boy: It sure is, and it's right near where we're going.

480.41

When you love a man he always smells good.

480.42

I go with a Can Can girl: Can I have this? . . . Can I have that? . . . Can I have a steak? . . . Can I have a drink? . . . Can I have a ring?

480.43

_____ shows his girl a lot of love and affection . . . he takes her to the drive-in movies, and lets her peek into the other cars.

480.44

"The engagement ring you gave me has always reminded me of a state capital," she said.

"Which one, dear?"

"Little Rock."

480.45

My brother's girl friend takes advantage of him. Every time he asks her to the movies, she asks him if she can bring a date.

480.46

The girl explained to her boyfriend that they would have difficulty in getting the blessing of her domineering mother. Determined his love for the girl would overcome all obstacles, he took her home and explained his intentions to his potential mother-in-law. The girl's mother was horrified at the thought and screeched, "I wouldn't dream of letting my daughter marry you! Frankly, I think you're effeminate."

"Yes," said the fellow thoughtfully, as he headed for the door, "compared to you, I probably am."

480.47

I love to kiss my girl behind the ears . . . cause that's where her lips are.

480.48

You're nobody until somebody loves you; next thing you know, you're a den mother.

480.49

Man: "Why did you call it love at second sight?"
Woman: "I didn't knew he was rich the first time."

LUCK

484.50

Loser—A man who gets a busy signal from a sea shell.

484.51

"I got terrible luck," said the businessman to the salesman. "I just lost $10,000 on a deal, my car was stolen, and my wife ran away with another man."

"That's nothing," said the salesman. "The other day I bought a suit with two pair of pants and today I burned a hole in the coat."

484.52

Bad luck: When 13 people you know are drinking in a bar and you're picking up the check.

484.53

Two years ago my wife had much better luck with her gardens. Nothing came up.

484.54

My boss is a great believer in luck. The harder he works, the more of it he seems to have.

484.55

Husband: "I was a fool to ever marry you."
Wife: "Yeah, but fools have all the luck."

MARRIAGE

494.01
Comedian Rodney Dangerfield said he "don't get no respect" with regard to anything. He said he carried his wife across the threshold of their first apartment, she looked at it, and said, "Don't put me down."

494.02
"That's a nice suit you have on," said Mr. Green to his friend. "Does your wife pick your clothes?"
  "No, just the pockets."

494.03
Bachelor: From the Latin baculum, a loose stick. Hence, an unattached man which a lady may stick to, or get stuck on.

494.04
Sam Levenson tells about the husband who argued and fought with his wife all day, and then moved to a hotel. But, by dinner time, he was hungry and lonely, so he called her.
  "Hello, Doris? What are you making for dinner?"
  "I'm making poison for dinner."
  "So only make one portion. I'm not coming home."

494.05
Joe was racked with sobs as they lowered his wife into her grave.
  "Don't cry, old sport," said his friend, consolingly. "In another year you'll meet another woman and get married again."
  "Another year," cried Joe, "what am I going to do tonight!"

494.06

"Pete," she said with her dying breath, "I haven't been a faithful wife. I'm the one who stole $5,000 from your safe. And I spent it all on your best friend that time I told you I was going to the Women's Club convention. Can you ever forgive me?"

"Don't give it a second thought," he answered. "I'm the one who poisoned you."

494.07

Husband: "If ever my wife and I argue, I make sure the children know nothing about it. I send them out for a walk."

Neighbor: "I see. They have nice rosy cheeks, haven't they?"

494.08

Divorces must have been invented the same time as marriages. Well, maybe a few months later.

494.09

Marriage starts with billing and cooing, and ends with billing and billing.

494.10

A lot of things puzzle married men. One of them is why all bachelors aren't stinking rich.

494.11

"People are saying that you and the husband aren't hitting it off the way you once did."

"Nonsense. We had a little spat and I shot him. But, really, that's all there was to it."

494.12

The wife had been observing the new neighbors across the street. She said to her husband, "Each time he comes home he hugs and kisses her on the porch. Why don't you do that?"

"Me?" he exclaimed. "I haven't even been introduced to her."

494.13

Marriage is like the Army: Everyone complains, but you'd be surprised at how many reenlist.

494.14

"A man got drunk at a party last night and proposed to me, and I'm so angry I can hardly control myself."

"Why does it make you so angry?"

"I'm already married to him."

494.15

"I'm what they call a suburban husband," remarked the exhausted commuter. "That's a gardener with sex privileges."

494.16

If you've half a mind to get married, do it. That's what it takes.

494.17

Martin was known among his friends for the punctuality with which he sent his wife her alimony payment each month. When asked the reason for his haste, he shivered and explained: "I'm afraid that if I should ever fall behind in my payments, she might decide to repossess me."

494.18
A hippie was getting married, so they gave the bride a shower an hour before she married.

494.19
The honeymoon is over when a man stops helping his wife with the dishes . . . and starts doing them himself.

494.20
Know what I did before I was married? . . . Anything I wanted to!

494.21
Zsa Zsa Gabor, who should know, once observed, "Husbands are like fires. They go out when unattended."

494.22
Any man who can keep his wife guessing for over a minute is probably dancing with her.

494.23
"Wife: "I'm so worried. My husband has been out all night, and I don't know where he is."
Friend: "Be happy. You'd be twice as miserable if you did know where he is."

494.24
"Mom," inquired a small boy, "why do all the fairy tales begin with 'Once upon a time'?"
"Oh, all of them don't," explained the surburban mother. "Some of them start off with 'I'm going to be working pretty late at the office tonight'."

494.25

A minister advertised for a handyman and next morning a neat young man rang the doorbell. "Well, young man," asked the minister, "can you start the fire and have breakfast ready by 7 o'clock?"

The young man thought he could.

"Can you polish all the silver and wash the dishes and keep the house and grounds tidy and neat?" was the next question.

"Look, Reverend," protested the young man. "I came here to see about getting married, but if it's going to be anything like that, you can count me out right now."

494.26

"My wife's a real pain. The least little thing sets her off."

"You're lucky. Mine's a self-starter."

494.27

A couple was leaving a party where the husband had slightly overcaroused.

"Dear," said his wife, "did anyone ever tell you that you were the most scintillating, fascinating, handsome, debonair man in the world?"

"No, I guess no one ever did," he replied.

"Then where did you get the idea?" she wanted to know.

494.28

If your wife is no longer suspicious when you come home late, it's later than you think.

494.29

Woman to detective: "I want my husband and the other woman followed day and night, and I want a complete report on what she sees in him."

494.30

Tom met Bill on the street and stopped to chat. "Why is it, Bill, you used to be so carefree and happy and, now that you're married, you're so grouchy?" Tom asked his friend.

"Well, when I was courting my wife she always talked about her buried treasure, so I proposed and she accepted," Bill related.

"But why should that make you grouchy?" asked the buddy.

"Because after we were married," Bill moaned, "I found out her buried treasure was her first husband."

494.31

A sweet young thing greeted the stockbroker as he entered a restaurant with his wife.

"Who was that?" demanded his wife.

"Forget about it," growled the financial wizard. "I'll have enough trouble explaining you to her."

494.32

A wife was so concerned about her husband's happiness that she hired three detectives to find out the reason for it.

494.33

"Please come right over," the man said to the undertaker. "My wife just dropped dead."

"Your wife?" said the funeral director, gravely. "I thought I buried her three years ago."

"That was my first wife," answered the bereaved husband. "I got married again."

"Oh," said the undertaker, "my heartiest congratulations."

494.34

Marriage is just another union that defies management.

494.35

"My wife is always asking me for money. Today she asked for $50, yesterday she wanted $75, and the day before that she had to have $200," said one man.

"What does she do with it?" asked a friend.

"I really don't know. I never give her any."

494.36

The best way to get your wife back from her mother's is to send her a copy of the local newspaper with one item cut out.

494.37

Two married men were talking. The first said, "I am very happy. I have a wonderful home, a great job, and the finest wife in the country."

His friend said, "Who wouldn't be happy with his wife in the country."

494.38

The marriages we regard as the happiest are those in which each of the partners believes that he or she got the best of it.

494.39

The lawyer for the plaintiff in a divorce case put his client on the stand.

"As I understand it," he said sympathetically, "you came home from a hard day's work each day for two weeks in a row and, instead of finding your wife alone and waiting for you, you found a different man in the closet each day?"

"That is correct," said the man.

"And this, of course, caused you untold unhappiness and anguish?"

"Darn right. I never had any room to hang up my clothes."

494.40

A husband reported this division of his income: 40 percent for food, 30 percent for shelter, and 50 percent for his wife's clothing and amusement. "But that makes 120 percent," his accountant protested.

"You don't have to tell me," sighed the husband, "I know it."

494.41

You know the honeymoon is over when he phones to say he'll be working late at the office and she has already written a note saying dinner is in the refrigerator.

494.42

"Daddy," said a little child, "does bigamy mean a man has one wife too many?"

The father answered, "Not necessarily, son. A man can have one wife too many and still not be a bigamist."

494.43

Newlywed discussing married life: "So far, all my wife can do is open cans and charge accounts."

494.44

A high school class at Prescott, Ark., voted on who was the happiest man in the world: the winner, "Mister Abby."

494.45

As they said about the x-ray specialist who married the homely girl: I wonder what he saw in her.

494.46

Marriage—The most expensive way to get your laundry done free.

494.47

A wedding caterer reminds his employees: Remember, we depend on repeat business. One out of every five brides gets married again.

494.48

A man I knew was married to a very hard woman. She kept telling him she hated him and couldn't wait until he died so she could walk on his grave. Finally he died, and they opened his will. It read, "Bury me at sea."

494.49

"Why do you insist on staring out the window all night?" asked the groom of his bride on their wedding night.

"Because," she said, "my mother told me my wedding night would be one of the most beautiful of my life, and I don't want to miss any of it."

494.50

Marriage is like a long feast. With the dessert first.

494.51

The perfect wife is one who is married to an ideal man. My own wife would be a good example.

494.52

"How nice to see you after all these years," said the lady to a former classmate. "You never married, did you, Mildred?"

"Oh, yes," the friend replied.

"But I remember after college when you broke off your engagement to that gorgeous football player, you said you wouldn't marry the finest man in the world even if he were rich and famous," said the lady.

"Well, I didn't," Mildred said.

494.53

A dear, sweet old lady was wandering about the wedding reception plucking Martinis from serving trays with the finesse of a grape picker. She came upon a well-dressed young man and, in her foggy condition, chirped, "You're the bridegroom, of course."

"No, I'm not," he answered wryly. "I was eliminated in the semifinals."

494.54

I just read that single people die earlier than married ones. It figures ... Haven't I always said that marriage is slow death?

494.55

Getting married is frequently like eating with a friend in a restaurant: When you see what the other fellow has you wish you'd taken that.

494.56

A man is incomplete until he's married. Then he's finished.

494.57

Wives are not like fishing buffs. They brag about the ones that got away and complain about the one they caught.

494.58

A fantastically henpecked husband finally did something entirely on his own initiative: He dropped dead. His nagging wife mourned his loss—and the fact that she had nobody left to badger. A visitor sympathized: "How you must miss dear Wilbur."

"Yes," said the widow wistfully, "it seems but yesterday that he stood at that very door, holding it open until two flies got in."

494.59

A marriage counselor reprimanded a lazy husband: "Aren't you ashamed to have your wife support you by taking in washing?"

"Yeah," said the husband, "but she's too dumb to do anything else!"

494.60

A husband is a man who starts out by giving a line and ends up by walking one.

494.61

"Do you," the minister asked, "take this woman for better or for worse, for richer or for poorer, through sickness and health, in good times and bad . . . "

"Please," the bride broke in, almost in tears, "you're going to talk him right out of it."

494.62

It seems to me most men flirt with the women they would not marry, and marry the women who would not flirt with them.

494.63

When a man and woman marry they become one. The trouble starts when they try to decide which one.

494.64

The placement officer asked, "Are you unmarried?"

The middle-aged woman replied, "Twice."

494.65

A happy marriage is when a couple is as deeply in love as they are in debt.

494.66

"My husband has no idea what I go through when he snores."

"Mine never misses his small change either."

494.67

Two fellows were discussing the vicissitudes of henpecked husbands.

"But let me tell you," said one, "I'm boss at my house. Last night I found there was no hot water. So I raised the roof. Believe me, I got hot water, too—in a hurry!"

There was a pause, and he added: "I hate to wash dishes in cold water, don't you?"

494.68

One husband was so henpecked that in order to go out with the boys he had to become a scoutmaster.

494.69

Wife: How lovely! Mrs. Jones is bringing in a yule log."
Husband: "Yeah—Jones."

494.70

A beautiful dancer once suggested to George Bernard Shaw that they marry. "Why just think," she said, "we could have a child with your brains and my looks."

"On the other hand," Shaw is said to have remarked, "we could have one with my looks and your brains."

494.71

A bride-to-be sighed to her mother, "There are so many things to do before the wedding—and I don't want to overlook the most insignificant detail."

"Don't worry," said her mother, "I'll see that he's there."

494.72

"I can't marry you," said the mountaineer justice of the peace. "This girl is only sixteen, so I'll have to see proof of parental consent."

"Parental consent!" screamed the potential groom. "Who do you think the guy with the rifle is, Davy Crockett?"

494.73

A battered boxer and his wife were in divorce court. The woman testified that her pug husband had beaten her day and night for the past 20 years.

"What do you have to say about this?" the judge sternly demanded.

The man replied, "Don't listen to her, your honor, she's punchy."

494.74

This chick's been married so many times, they don't play "Here Comes the Bride" ... They play "I Love a Parade."

494.75

A happy home is one in which each spouse grants the possibility that the other may be right, though neither believes it.

494.76

Old-fashioned girl: One who has never been kissed by her ex-husband.

494.77

He: "Then it's all set. We elope at midnight?"

She: "Yes, darling."

He: Are you sure you have everything packed in your suitcase?"

She: "I'm positive. Papa and mamma helped me."

494.78

There is an ongoing dispute about whether or not to marry a beautiful girl or a homely one. Well, there's one thing about a homely girl—if she leaves, you probably won't feel as bad.

494.79

A bedraggled, henpecked husband finally snuck off to an office party once and had the time of his life. But, about 11 p.m., he got roaring drunk and passed out. He woke up at 4 a.m. and panicked.

So he called his wife and said, "Don't pay the ransom, dear, I've escaped."

494.80

"I was a fool when I married you!" shouted the wife during a connubial spat.

"Of course you were," replied the angry husband, "but I was so infatuated with you that I didn't even notice."

494.81

The young bridegroom was deliriously happy. As he and his beautiful bride strolled along the shore in the moonlight he felt the urge of poetry stirring from within and recited, "Roll on, thou deep and dark blue ocean, roll."

"Oh, darling," gushed the awed bride. "How wonderful you are. It's doing it."

494.82

The honeymoon is over when she complains about the racket he makes while he fixes his own breakfast.

494.83

The husband said to the marriage counselor: "It all started when she wanted her mother in the wedding picture."

494.84

A Frenchman came to the United States for the first time and was invited to a golden wedding anniversary. Not understanding the ritual, he asked a friend, "For what is this celebration?"

"Well, do you see those two old people?" asked the friend. "They've been together 50 years and now they're celebrating their golden wedding."

"Oui!" exclaimed the Frenchman. "I see. He's been living with the lady for 50 years and now he married her. A magnificent gesture!"

494.85

Marriage: A new leash on life.

494.86

"You absolutely promised that after we were married you would never look at another woman," said the wife.

"Oh, well," he replied, "I thought you understood that that was only a campaign promise."

494.87

My wife doesn't believe in shouting at me . . . she believes she can get better results with a low nerve-racking whine.

494.88

Doctor: "I don't like the looks of your husband."
Wife: "Neither do I, but he's very good with the children."

494.89

"Guess what, Dad," said the aspiring young actor, "I've got my first part in a play. I'm playing a man who has been married for 20 years."

"That's good, son. Keep at it and soon you'll get a speaking part," advised the father.

494.90

The handsome young minister said to the pretty member of the congregation, "You should see our new altar at the church."

The girl replied, "Lead me to it."

494.91

Alimony: An expensive yet soothing medicine prescribed by a judge for a divorcee's bleeding heart.

MATERNITY
BIRTH CONTROL

500.50
"I'm sorry," said the boss, "but if I give you two hours for lunch today I'd have to do the same thing for every employee whose wife gave birth to quintuplets."

500.51
The anxious father was pacing up and down outside the maternity ward. Then the nurse came out and he quickly asked: "Is it a boy?"

She answered, "The next to the last one was."

500.52
A mother-to-be was showing the pink dresses she bought for her expected baby.

"What will you do if it's a boy?" asked a neighbor.

"In that case, he'll wear the dresses and I'll teach him to fight."

500.53
Joe and Jim, both waiting for their first child to arrive, paced the hospital waiting room floor nervously.

"Boy," said Joe, "this had to happen on my vacation."

"That's not so bad," said Jim. "I'm on my honeymoon."

500.54
A woman called her insurance company to ask her representative to alter her family policy. "I have just had twins," she told him.

The man had trouble hearing the woman, and said, "Will you please repeat that?"

"Not if I can help it," she replied.

500.55

When it comes to birth control, you just can't beat a good fight!

500.56

Salesman to wife who had just presented him with triplets: "My dear, a sample would have been sufficient. There is no necessity for carrying them in stock."

500.57

The owner of a dress shop framed this complaint letter he received. Addressed to "The Big Store" it said, "Dear Mr. B. Store: Please cancel my order for maternity dress, Model 61, which you were supposed to deliver three weeks ago. My delivery turned out faster than yours."

500.58

It was going-home day, and the salesman ushered his wife and their newborn quadruplets into the house. Besides the older children, grandparents, uncles, aunts, and even neighbors were on hand to greet the new arrivals. Everyone made all the appropriate comments except the family's five-year-old son. He stood there looking quizzically at the blanket-wrapped bundles and then added a comment of his own: "We'd better start calling people right away," he said. "They're gonna be harder to get rid of than kittens."

MATHEMATICS

502.50

The shortest distance between two points is usually under construction.

502.51

Teacher: "If you substract 19 from 46, what is the difference?"

Pupil: "Uh, well ... that's what I say, what's the difference?"

502.52

The teacher asked little Jimmy how he would go about dividing 5 potatoes among 15 people.

"I'd cook 'em and mash 'em!"

502.53

A teacher asked one of her second-graders what one and one was. He replied, "One and one—that's a ball and a strike."

502.54

Two wizened old fishermen had an argument over which was better at figurin'. A friend proposed this problem: If a crew caught 500 pounds of cod and sold it at 3 cents a pound, how much would they receive?

The two brooded and pondered, but neither could come up with an answer. Finally one gent asked that the problem be repeated.

"Wait a minute," he cried, "did you say cod . . ?"

"Yes," said the friend.

"No wonder I couldn't figure it, I thought you said salmon."

502.55

An Iowa teacher was giving her class an arithmetic test. She asked the question: "If a farmer had 5,000 bushels of wheat to market at a dollar a bushel, what would he get?"

A hand quickly shot up and its owner said, "A government loan."

502.56

A clever teacher asked, "If there were three flies on the table, and I swatted one, how many would be left?"

An equally clever second-grader replied, "One, the dead one."

502.57

A rural painter drew a landscape of a friend's fields and house, but he took occasional artistic license in order to make a better picture. The farmer took one look at the picture, turned, and said: "Yes, sir. It looks just like the place—and thanks for trimming the hedges."

502.58

A sophomore class in geometry was examining a complicated proof of the Pythagorean Theorem. The teacher asked a pupil whether they had proved the theorem. He replied, "I don't know if we've proved it, but I think we've rendered it highly probable."

MEMORY

514.50

Nothing is quite as responsible for the good old days as a bad memory.

514.51

Wife: "Dear, do you have a good memory for faces?"
Husband: "Yes, pretty good."
Wife: "Boy, am I glad to hear that. I just broke your shaving mirror."

514.52

An elderly woman in a small Midwestern town called her bank to arrange for the disposition of a large bond left to her. The banker asked her: "Is this bond for conversion or redemption?"

After a long pause, the voice came back: "Sonny, I forgot. Is this the First National Bank or the first parish church?"

514.53

I went to see a psychiatrist about amnesia last week and he made me pay in advance.

514.54

Two friends were chatting in a bar about their wives' foibles and idiosyncracies. "Why is it," said one, "that husbands always forget wedding anniversaries, and wives remember them?"

"Let me give you an analogy," said his friend. "Do you remember the biggest fish you ever caught?"

"Sure," the other replied.

"Do you think the fish remembers?"

MEN

516.50

Joe E. Lewis, the comedian, says: "Show me a man with both feet on the ground, and I'll show you a man who can't get his pants on."

516.51

Two bachelors started talking about cooking, and one said, "I bought a cookbook once, but never used it. Too much trouble."

"Why was that?" his friend asked.

He answered, "All the recipes started off with 'Take a clean dish'."

516.52

Male: About the only thing left you can't get from a mail-order house.

516.53

All it takes to separate the men from the boys is the girls.

516.54

Bachelor—One who's foot loose and fiancée free.

516.55

A gentleman looks at a beautiful woman without lust. A gentleman is a darned fool.

516.56

Angry father: "What's the idea, young man, bringing in my daughter at two o'clock in the morning?"

Suitor: "It started to rain."

MISTAKE

524.40

A man was stretched out in the street with no one paying attention. Finally, a young woman came along and, in a flash, fell beside him and began applying mouth-to-mouth resuscitation.

"This is great, honey," he whispered, "but hold off until I finish wiring this manhole."

524.41

I loved the battle scenes. I haven't seen such fighting and yelling and screaming and violence since I got on a school bus by mistake!

524.42

A friend suggested that we run the following: "If you find a mistake in this magazine it was put there on purpose. We try to publish something for everybody, and some people seem to look only for mistakes."

524.43

A Yale student remarked: "Architects cover their mistakes with ivy. A bride covers hers with mayonnaise."

524.44

Bachelor: A man who never makes the same mistake once.

524.45

Judge: "You admit that you stole the fruit from this man's market?"
Defendant: "Actually, your honor, I took it by mistake."
Judge: "How's that?"
Defendant: "I thought it was fresh."

524.46

The man who claims he never made a mistake in his life generally has a wife who did.

524.47

During World War II a young airman landed on an aircraft carrier and, as he climbed out of the cockpit, exclaimed: "What a day! I shot down seven Zeroes, sank a destroyer, and torpedoed a battleship!"

"Velly good," came the reply, "but you make one rittle mistake."

524.48

Andrew Carnegie was showing some people through one of his plants one day when he stopped to talk to an old employee. "And how long have you been with us?" asked the industrialist.

"Thirty-nine years," said the man, "and in all that time I have made only one small error."

"That's very good," Carnegie said, "but in the future let's try to be a bit more careful."

524.49

Have you ever read a copy of True Confessions? It's full of stories about girls who made mistakes . . . and the advertisements all tell the girls how to be beautiful, so they can get in on some of those mistakes.

524.50

A beautiful blonde ran away from her small town home and joined the circus. The first thing she did was to tell the ringmaster, "I know I'm new, but I don't want to make the usual beginner's mistakes. Can you give me a few helpful hints?"

"Well, I guess so," said the ringmaster, "first off, don't get undressed around the bearded lady."

524.51

There is nothing that can replace experience. It's the one thing that allows you to recognize a mistake when you have made it again.

MORALS
MORALITY

534.50

The store clerk held the suspicious-looking five-dollar bill up to the light and said, "I'm sorry, miss, but this bill is counterfeit."

"Good grief," said the gorgeous blonde, "I've been seduced."

534.51

Bachelor—A man who comes to work each morning from a different direction.

534.52

All this talk about the immorality of actors is nonsense. They're just more honestly sinful than others.

534.53

Evangelist at revival meeting: "Adultery is worse than murder! Isn't that so, Sister Jones?"

Sister Jones: "I can't rightly say. I never killed anybody."

534.54

"Yes, your honor, I did go to the hotel with this man. But I couldn't help it. He deceived me."

"How did he do that?"

"He told the hotel clerk that I was his wife."

534.55

Discovering a virgin nowadays is kind of like a parking space in New York City. There are damned few left and just when you think you've spotted one, some guy moves in ahead of you.

534.56

Give me chastity and self-restraint, but do not give it yet.

534.57

A man about town was playing a game of hypothetical questions with a naïve young model. He asked, "Would you spend the weekend with a total stranger for a million dollars?" The lovely girl thought it over momentarily and, being of a mercenary nature, she answered, "Yes."

"And what if one offered you 50 dollars?" he asked. Her face somewhat flushed, the model snapped back, "Just what do you think I am?"

"That has been established," teased the man. "Now, I'm trying to determine the degree."

MUSIC
DANCING   SINGING

542.50
I have come to this conclusion about all these new dances ... if you don't end up with a slipped disc, you're not doing it right.

542.51
How monotonous the sounds of the forest would be if the music came only from the Top Ten birds.

542.52
My neighbors must really like my piano playing ... just last week, they broke all the front room windows, so they could hear better.

542.53
My son has two motives when he plays his trumpet—pleasure and revenge.

542.54
A folk singer is someone who sings about the joys of the simple life—using a $5,000 sound system.

542.55
A henpecked husband was escorting his wife to a concert. They arrived shortly after the performance had begun.
"What are they playing?" asked the wife of one of the attendants.
"The Fifth Symphony," came the answer.
She then turned on her husband. "You dumb cluck! We've already missed four of them!"

542.56

A matron had just finished singing "Chicago" at a women's club show, and a man in the back of the audience was observed gently sobbing.

"Oh, you must be from the Windy City," said the woman.

"No," he replied. "I'm a musician."

542.57

The piano teacher addressed a particularly unruly pupil: "I'm warning you. If you don't behave, I'm going to tell your parents you have talent."

NAMES

546.50

A dapper executive stood in the baggage waiting room while the plane disgorged his luggage. His wife who had come to the airport to drive him home stood by.

A curvaceous airline hostess swiveled by and the executive called to her, "I hope we fly together again soon, Miss Radcliff."

"How do you know her name?" demanded his wife.

"Oh, it's posted in the plane under the names of the captain and copilot."

"I see," said the wife. "Now tell me the names of the captain and copilot."

546.51

A woman appeared before St. Peter at the Pearly Gates. "I'm Mrs. Smith and I'm looking for my husband," she announced.

"We have a lot of Smiths," the saint replied. "Could you be more specific?"

"Well, he said that if I were ever untrue to him he'd turn in his grave!"

"Oh, you're looking for 'Pinwheel' Smith," said St. Peter.

546.52

A sweet young thing was on a sight-seeing tour of Detroit, and the guide was calling out places of interest.

"On the left," said the man, "is the Dodge House."

"John Dodge?" asked the girl.

"No, Horace Dodge," said the guide.

Continuing on the tour, he announced, "On the right, the Ford House."

"Henry?" asked the girl.

"No, lady, Edsel."

Further on he said, "On the left is Christ's Church."

"Jesus? Or did I blow it again?" asked the girl.

546.53

The reason I mention my name so often is that it may be necessary later to identify the body.

546.54

A man named Jim Smith claimed that he knew every important man in the world. He mentioned the fact once too often, and a friend, fed up, finally said, "I'll bet you $100,000 that you don't know the President, John Wayne, and the Pope." Smith took the bet.

First they flew off to Hollywood and went to John Wayne's house. The Duke opened the door and said, "Hi, Jim, how's everything?"

Then they went off to Washington, and got a similar greeting from the President. Then off to Rome. Smith went into the papal residence, and a few moments later appeared on the balcony overlooking Vatican Square with the Pope. Thinking it was a fraud, his friend turned to a local visitor and said, pointing to the balcony, "Who is that?" The native replied, "I don't know who the little Italian fellow is, but the other one is Jim Smith."

NATIONALITY

554.50

An Australian and a Texan were going at it over the relative merits of each locality. The Texan bragged that Texas had the biggest men, the biggest prairies, the biggest ranches, and the biggest cattle in the whole world.

Just then a kangaroo hopped by, and the Australian remarked, "Don't mind that. Another one of those pesky grasshoppers."

554.51

After the Czechoslovakian invasion by Russia, one Czech was reported as saying, "We must be the most neutral country in the world, we don't even intervene in our own internal affairs."

554.52

Most Czechoslovakians were not overly pleased with their communist government, and it became somewhat of a standard joke among Czechs that the only good thing about it was that the Slovaks had to put up with it, too.

554.53

A friend of mine went into a Chinese restaurant recently and broke a tooth on a fortune cookie. The message read, "Best to you under our new president, Ghenghis Khan."

554.54

A Frenchman once said to Mark Twain, "When an American has nothing else to do, he can always spend a few years trying to find out who his grandfather was."

"Quite right," said Twain, "and when all other interests fail for a Frenchman, he can always try to find out who his father was."

OPINION

562.50
Some people think the world is round ... I think it's crooked!

562.51
Author: "What is your exact opinion of my new novel?"
Critic: "It is absolutely worthless."
Author: "I suspected that, but give it to me anyway."

562.52
Public opinion—What people think other people are thinking.

562.53
Two privates were talking about their sergeant. Said the first, "Sergeant Jones is a real pain in the neck."

"Do you think so?" asked his friend. "I have a much lower opinion of him."

562.54
Don't think harshly of her. She's just as God made her, even if at times she's a great deal worse.

562.55
A lady tourist was admiring a necklace on display in the Indian village. "What are those things?" she asked.

"Alligator teeth," explained the Indian.

After recovering her composure, she said, "Well, I suppose that they hold the same meaning for you as pearls do for us."

"Not quite, lady," he answered. "Anybody can open an oyster."

PEACE
WAR

572.50
During the "Six Day War" between Israel and Egypt, an Israeli soldier asked his girl for a date.

"Don't you know there's a war going on?" she asked.

"Oh yeah. Well, how about the weekend?"

572.51
The United States has had an interesting 10 years in Southeast Asia. It's been like stepping into a wading pool that's 80 feet deep.

572.52
The President told us last year that he could end the war. Now, he's told us how. And we can hardly wait for next year, when he tells us when.

572.53
Neutral: A country that will not sell munitions to those at war unless they pay in advance.

572.54
During the London blitz, a wife screamed, "Come on, Fred, we've got to head for the air raid shelter."

"I'm not going until I find my false teeth," came the reply.

"Are you balmy?" she asked. "They're not dropping sandwiches."

PERSONALITY

580.50
I'd rather be a popular idiot than a successful smart aleck.

580.51
He's got the personality of an old manhole cover.

580.52
He's so disagreeable that he can make enemies at a Dale Carnegie class.

PHILOSOPHY

584.50

A philosopher is a person who doesn't care which side his bread is buttered on; he knows he eats both sides anyway.

584.51

The worst thing about any philosophy, good or bad, is that it has absolutely no control over who believes in it.

584.52

Two angels were sitting lazily on a cloud, and one said to the other, "I've never asked you much about philosophy, but tell me, do you believe in the heretofore?"

584.53

A descendant of a nobleman was taunting Heraclitus about his low birth.

The philosopher replied, "The difference between us is that your family ends with you and mine begins with me."

POLITICS
POLITICIANS

592.30
A successful politician is someone who can rock the boat himself and then convince his constituency that there is a hurricane blowing.

592.31
My grandfather was one of the best politicians in this state, my father was renowned in the political field, and I don't plan to work either.

592.32
My brother-in-law said that politics in his home town were so crooked that if a man said he controlled 20 votes he was just talking about himself.

592.33
A statesman is a man who plays both ends against the muddle.

592.34
Two state legislators were lamenting the recent death of a colleague. "I understand our friend left very few effects," said one.

"Only fitting," said the other. "He had very few causes."

592.35
Eugene Field once told of a large group of state legislators who were on a train when it was stopped by bandits. "After relieving the bandits of their cash and valuables," Field said, "the legislators proceeded on their journey with increased enthusiasm and joie de vivre."

592.36

"What did the gathering do, Senator, when you told them you've never paid a cent for a vote and never intended to?"

"Well, I'll tell you, a half dozen or so applauded, but most of them got up and walked out."

592.37

"Let's run a clean campaign," said the politician to his opponent.

"Okay," said the other, "you promise not to lie about the Democrats and I'll promise not to tell the truth about the Republicans."

592.38

I don't know about the State Department. With all these goodwill trips, why don't we have any?

592.39

The congressman was admiring his new son and observed, "He'll be a great politician one of these days. Look how easy he wriggles out of things."

592.40

The local election was near, and one old resident asked a relative newcomer what he thought of the two candidates running for mayor.

"I'm glad," said the man, "that only one of them can be elected."

592.41

A politician who had changed his mind on a crucial issue was congratulated by a colleague. "I'm glad you saw the light," he said.

Replied the other, "I didn't. I felt the heat."

592.42

Some sage once remarked, "If you live in a town that is run by a committee, you had better be on it."

592.43

"Daddy, what's a 'liberal Republican'?"
"Wait, son, I'll look it up."
"But, Dad, that's the Encyclopedia of Mythology."
"I know, son, I know."

592.44

Two congressional secretaries were chatting over lunch at Capitol Hill. Said one, "Do you like conceited politicians as much as the other kind?"
"What other kind?" said her friend.

592.45

My wife (girl) thought she would write to her Congressman, but she didn't know whether he could read.

592.46

Politician: One who is like a poor relative. You hear from them only when they need help.

592.47

One Senator to another: "You spend a billion here, a billion there, and the first thing you know, it adds up."

592.48

"I suppose," said the candidate, "the proper thing for me to do in this election is to stand on my record."
"No," advised the political boss, "stand on the other fellow's."

592.49

A politician was campaigning for office in New York City, and was speaking one day in Chinatown. He carried on for about half an hour on the great merits of the Chinese people, their many contributions to the city, and ways they could benefit if he were elected.

After the speech, the floor was opened to questions. One reporter said, "Sir, after that speech, what chance does your opponent have in this area?"

Cocksure and full of fire, the politician boomed, "He doesn't have a Chinaman's chance."

592.50

In politics, if you're against it, it's a machine; if you're for it, it's a party.

592.51

God bless the President, the Governor, and the Mayor—if they're worth it.

592.52

Adlai Stevenson said he was once embarrassed by a sign he noticed in the crowd to which he was to deliver a campaign speech. It read "Stevenson's the man," and was being carried by an obviously pregnant woman.

592.53

"Here's what we do," said the cannibal chief. "We leak word that our government is unstable. The Russians will immediately make overtures. Naturally the Americans will get worried and begin relations. Then the Russians will ask to send ambassadors. The Americans will ask for equal representation. We invite them both to send emissaries. And when they get here we eat 'em."

592.54

A politician got into some trouble with his campaign slogan. It read, "Future lies ahead."

592.55

During the regime of one of the unpopular rulers of Vietnam in the mid-sixties, it was said that someone broke into the President's quarters in Saigon one night and stole the entire results of the next free election.

592.56

Under the capitalist system, man exploits man. Under communism, it's vice versa.

592.57

The time many a politician stumps his state is after it has elected him.

592.58

Any man who can double his salary before he gets the job, deserves to be President.

592.59

Muriel Humphrey once noted that losing builds character, but said that her husband Hubert feels he could build an awful lot of character out of winning.

592.60

"Being Vice President," says Spiro T. Agnew, "is like adding maternity benefits to Social Security—you're there, but nobody needs you."

592.61

Radical—An unemployed conservative.

592.62

Statesman—A politician who has retired or passed away.

592.63

Comedian Lou Ritchie said he once saw an authentic Latin band—they were constantly changing leaders.

592.64

Governor Al Smith was once in a hurry to get to a radio station to make a broadcast. He tried to get a cab, but the driver, not recognizing him, asked to be excused so he could go home and listen to the speech.

Flattered, Smith produced a five-dollar bill. "Hop in," said the cabbie, "the hell with the governor."

POVERTY

602.50

Beggars should be abolished. It annoys one to give to them; and it annoys one not to give to them.

602.51

A bum on the street panhandled a dollar from a wealthy man, but the man told the bum to be sure and spend it on food.

The bum replied, "My good man, do I tell you how to spend your money?"

602.52

The old Indian chief had been around the world with traveling shows, and had known many famous people. During an interview he was reminded of his humble origins when a reporter asked if, when he was a child on the plains, he had lived in a hide lean-to.

"No," he answered, "but we moved into one as soon as my folks could afford it."

602.53

My brother-in-law told me he is worried that the war on poverty will end before he finds out where he can surrender.

602.54

A woman waiting for a ride noticed a poor, slovenly man walking by. Touched, but tactful, she bent over, then stood up, put a quarter in his hand, and said, "Pardon me, but did you drop this?"

"Well, how about that," said the man taking the coin, "a lot of people would've kept that for themselves."

602.55

There was an old woman who lived in a shoe. She had so many children her welfare check came to $4,892.

602.56

As a bum watched a chauffeured millionaire drive by in his limousine, he said to himself, "But for me, there go I."

602.57

"Tell me," said the sympathetic man to the beggar, "how did you get yourself into such circumstances?"

"Well," replied the derelict, "when I had the world by the tail, I let go to reach for the moon."

PRESS
PUBLICITY

612.50

"It seems to me your opinions on this subject have undergone a change, sir," the newscaster said.

"Of course not," replied the senator.

"But these are not the same views you expressed some time ago," the broadcaster pointed out.

"Those were not my views," the lawmaker snorted, "those were my interviews."

612.51

No person has ever found perfect accuracy in a newspaper account of a happening which he witnessed.

612.52

"What!" screamed the managing editor to the cub reporter. "You mean there's no story about the senator arriving in town?"

"Not a thing," said the lad, "the train crashed."

612.53

In the late fall, a bum, covered with newspapers, was sleeping on a park bench. He rolled slightly and said, "Now is when you appreciate the Times' fuller coverage."

612.54

A friend of mine called the local newspaper the other day and told them he normally didn't complain about his newspaper landing on the roof, but now he has an apartment on the second floor of a 37-story building.

PROFANITY

622.50

The devil was sitting next to the phone, it rang, he picked it up and said, "Hell, yes."

622.51

The prosperous merchant decided to go to church for a change. After the service he enthusiastically shook the minister's hand and said, "That was a damned fine sermon you gave, Reverend, damned fine!"

"I'm pleased you liked it," said the preacher, "but I do wish you would refrain from using those terms to express yourself."

"I can't help expressing myself, Reverend," said the businessman. "I still think it was a damned good sermon. I liked it so much I put a 50-dollar bill in the collection plate."

Looking him squarely in the eye, the minister shot back, "The hell you did!"

622.52

Wife: "All night long you were cursing me in your sleep. You swore a blue streak."
Husband: "Who was sleeping?"

622.53

A farmer known for his rich, flowing profanity, was reprimanded by the local preacher who was able to get a promise that he would stop. One day the preacher decided to visit the fellow in the fields to see if he were living up to his vows. As the parson approached, unseen by the farmer, the mules pulling the plow struck a stubborn streak. The farmer let loose with several choice profanities and was about to continue with some more when, out of the corner of his eye, he spotted the preacher. "That's what I would've said," he quickly blurted, "before I got religion. Now, would you nice animals please giddyup!"

622.54

My mother-in-law came home yesterday and said, "I almost ran over a man, and I think he was from Florida. When he got to the curb he said something about the sun and the beach."

PSYCHOLOGY

634.50

Psychological warfare is a husband saying, "You want equal rights? Okay—*you* kill the mouse!"

634.51

Psychologist—A man who, when a pretty blonde enters, watches everybody else.

634.52

The psychologist was putting the new job applicants through one of his dreamed-up tests which involved carving objects out of soap. As the test was progressing, he walked from one person to another to see what they were making. The to-be-expected objects were seen to be emerging—an animal, car, house, flower, etc.—until he came to one applicant whose work defied description. "What's this?" he asked.

"Soap flakes," replied the practical testee.

RELIGION

656.20

Jimmy was on his way to church and Mom gave him two dimes.

"One is for the collection basket," said Mom, "and one is for ice cream."

A few blocks from church Jimmy dropped one of the coins and it rolled through a grating.

"Sorry, God," said Jimmy, looking upwards, "there goes your dime."

656.21

Church members are either pillars or caterpillars. The pillars hold up the church; the caterpillars just crawl in and out.

656.22

A preacher whose congregation usually occupied only the back pews in the church was surprised to find a lone man, a stranger, sitting in the front pew. After the service, he asked the man why he chose a front seat.

The man said he was a bus driver, and wanted to see firsthand how to get people to sit in the rear.

656.23

The average man's idea of a good sermon is one that goes over his head and hits a neighbor.

656.24

A small child swallowed a coin, and his parents naturally became quite concerned. "Send for the doctor," said the mother.

"Heck no," said the father. "I'm sending for the pastor, he can get money out of anybody."

656.25

The maid had been secretly using the bathtub of her employer, an elderly bishop. He was a bachelor, very particular about his toilet, and desired exclusive use of the tub.

He scolded the woman indignantly. "What irritates me the most, Margaret, is that you did all this behind my back!"

656.26

The pastor announced that he planned to make some improvements in the church, starting with a chandelier. This brought opposition from the old-timer in the back of the congregation.

When the priest asked why he opposed, the man explained:

"Well, first, no one can spell it. So how are you going to order it? Second, no one can play it if we do get it. And third, what we really need around here is more light!"

656.27

On one of those block letter signs common to many New England churches was the topic for Sunday's sermon: "Do you know what hell is?" Underneath was scribbled, "Come and hear our organist."

656.28

Religion should be a constant and beautiful tabernacle in the mind and the heart; not something you visit once a week.

656.29

"There aren't many people here in church," said one girl to another.

"Right," agreed her friend. "Sometimes the congregation is so small that when the reverend says, 'Dearly beloved,' you think you are being proposed to."

656.30

Some clergymen are really getting with the times. One put up a sign that read: "Redemption Center—No Stamps Needed." Another sign read, "Come early if you want a back seat."

656.31

Religion, through a kid's eye, is not always seen the same as grownups see—or hear—it. The Reverend Dale Lind, of New York City, cites some examples brought to his attention: "Harold be they name"; "Give us this day our jelly bread"; "Lead us not into Penn Station"; "Deliver us from people"; and "As shepherds washed their socks by night."

656.32

A beautiful young girl stood up at a revival meeting and shouted, "Hallelujah. Yesterday I was in the arms of Satan and today I'm in the arms of the Savior!"

A voice from the back then asked, "What are you doing tomorrow?"

656.33

The preacher was talking to the organist. "I'm going to ask everyone who would like to help pay off the mortgage to stand. Meanwhile, you play appropriate music."

"Nearer My God to Thee?"

"No, the Star Spangled Banner."

SAFETY

666.50

(Safety Hint) ... While driving at night, when approaching an oncoming auto, dim your headlights ... if you don't have any headlights, turn up your radio real loud.

666.51

And now for our safety tip of the week: While out driving, beware of the reckless, irresponsible, road hog speeder— especially if it's you!

666.52

Nothing brings the traffic regulations to mind quite like spotting a police car in the rear view mirror.

666.53

A safety belt is the best way to keep from leaving the scene of an accident.

SALES
SALESMAN

672.30

Salesman: "Are you sure your boss isn't in his office?"
Receptionist: "Are you doubting his word?"

672.31

A shy young salesman hesitantly approached the receptionist. "I'd like to see Mr. Brown," he said.

"I'm sorry, but Mr. Brown is out just now. Would you care to make an appointment for some other time?"

"No," the young man replied. "I'll just stop by later." He started to walk away, and then returned to ask, "By the way, can you tell me when he'll be out again?"

672.32

Salesmen must have the philosophy which is attributed to the U.S. Marine Corps. They never retreat; they may at times march to the rear, but never retreat.

672.33

In a sales meeting: "You show me the man who has the moral fiber to lose a $10,000 order and keep smiling ... and I'll show you an idiot."

672.34

A salesman covering a large territory was complaining to his sales manager of the many hours his selling and traveling involved.

"Why," replied the sales manager, "when I was out on the road, I often put in sixteen hours a day and thought nothing of it."

"I've been doing the same thing for weeks, and I don't think a lot of it either," replied the salesman.

672.35

Mrs.: "What's happening at the church? There's such a large crowd!"

Mr.: "There's a traveling salesman down there confessing his sins."

672.36

"I got two orders today," declared the new salesman.

"Splendid," said the boss. "What were they?"

"One was 'Get out,' and the other was 'Stay out'."

672.37

The salesman was urging a small country storekeeper to carry his full product line.

"I can't afford it," the retailer declared. "I owe everybody, now."

The salesman insisted, "But you owe it to yourself to carry a line like ours which can bring you greater profits."

"I know it," agreed the prospect, "but I'm not pushing myself like my other creditors are."

672.38

"My birthstone is the opal," said the salesman's daughter to her father—with more than a hint of suggestion in her voice. "What's yours?"

"Mine's the grindstone," replied the father meaningfully.

672.39

Today's supermarket sells almost everything, but if you find automobile tires among the groceries, you're in the wrong place. That's the drugstore.

672.40

My brother-in-law went to a big fire sale last week and bought a big fire.

672.41

A salesman always kept his hat on while doing "desk work" at the office. When kidded about it, he answered, "That's to remind me I really ought not to be there!"

672.42

The auto salesman announced to his son there would soon be a new baby in the house.

"I suppose," said the little fellow, "that means I'll have to be traded in."

672.43

As the perfume saleslady said to the pretty young customer, "Don't buy this brand if you are bluffing."

672.44

A door-to-door salesman was trying to sell a vacuum cleaner to a housewife, but she said that, while she wasn't interested, he should try next door. "We often borrow theirs and it's in horrible condition."

672.45

A man who lived in Scarsdale, N. Y., and worked for a large advertising agency in the city could not understand the awe and admiration shown him by the neighborhood children. Finally one day one of the toddlers shied up to him and asked, "Are you really a space salesman?"

672.46

A brush salesman knocked on a screen door which presented a tableau of a nine-year-old boy agonizingly practicing his piano lessons.

"Is your mommy home?" asked the salesman.

"What do you think?" said the kid.

672.47

A salesman returned home unexpectedly and found a man in the closet. "What're you doing here?" he asked. The fellow replied, "Well, everybody's gotta be somewhere!"

672.48

The shoe salesman was stunned when the shapely girl he had been waiting on slapped his face and tore out of the store.

"What in blazes happened?" roared the boss.

"I don't know," replied the puzzled clerk. "All I said to her was, 'These shoes will make street walking a pleasure'."

672.49

"It's actually a fire sale," said the tired, worn-looking salesman. "If I don't make a sale, I'm fired."

672.50

Recession—A time when sales are down 5 percent and staff meetings are up 25 percent.

672.51

Here's a salesman with a real problem. He received a note in the mail that said: "If you don't stop making love to my wife, I'll shoot you." The trouble is, there was no signature.

672.52

A real estate man applied pressure to make a sale of some poor farmland. "All this land needs," he pointed out to his prospect, "is a little water, a cool breeze and some good people to settle here."

"Maybe so," said the wary buyer, "but that's all Hell needs, too."

672.53

The salesman for a drug company rushed into the research laboratory waving a clipping. He found the head of the department and demanded to know how he was expected to sell the company's life-preserving tonic when it wouldn't do the job it was supposed to do. "See," he shouted, "it says right here in the paper that this 98-year-old woman died. And I happen to know she was taking our tonic!"

"Let me see it," said the department head. He studied the clipping for a moment and then commented: "I guess you're right, but all is not lost. Did you notice here where it says they saved the baby?"

672.54

A Boise salesman had to go to New York on business, and his wife asked if she could come along.

"But I'll be tied up in conference all the time. You wouldn't enjoy it at all."

"Oh, that's all right. I can spend all my time shopping for clothes."

"That's silly. You can get anything you want right here."

"Oh, wonderful. That's what I hoped you would say."

672.55

I knew a traveling salesman who died and left his family 65,000 towels.

672.56

Two salesmen met by chance in a bar and began throwing the bull.

"I'm from Detroit, in the paper business," said one, "and just yesterday I sold 50,000 cardboard boxes to General Motors."

"I'm from Wappingers Falls," said the other, "and I work for a clothing store. Two days ago a woman came in and asked for a suit to bury her husband in. And I sold her two pairs of pants."

672.57

It had been a particularly trying day for the salesman and he was looking forward to a nice hot bath, a relaxing evening, and an early bedtime. This proved to be mere wishful thinking, since he no sooner walked in the door of his home than his wife reminded him about a cocktail party they had to attend that evening.

The tired salesman endured the party until the wee hours of the dawn. At that point he could take it no longer. Standing up, he remarked to a fellow party-goer:

"I'm completely bushed. Guess it's time for me to go flirt with some good-looking blonde so my wife will take me home."

672.58

A salesman's showing of a house was interrupted by the prospective buyer, who asked, "Is it always this damp?"

"Of course," he enthused. "And think what an advantage that is in case of a fire."

672.59

The real estate salesman spent all day Saturday showing a young couple through mobile homes.

"Now this one," he said wearily, "has a hobby room. Do you have any hobbies?"

"Yes," said the wife, "looking through mobile homes on Saturday."

672.60

A sales manager with a large sales force kept track of his men by sticking a pin in a large map behind his desk at the point where each salesman should be. One of them, he noted, had produced no sales for several weeks. Summoning him to the home office he gave him a combination dressing down and pep talk. Ending up, he said: "I didn't call you here, Abernathy, to tell you that your job is in jeopardy, but if you'll look at the map behind my desk, you'll notice I've loosened your pin!"

672.61

A salesman walked into a firm office and was offered a cigar by the purchasing agent. "Just had a baby!" explained the agent. The salesman took the proffered cheroot, sat down, and lit up.

Then he said, "Large family, I presume."

672.62

"To make it in sales these days, a man has to be part psychologist," boasted a salesman. "Not only do you have to outguess and outthink the other fellow, you have to be able to know exactly what's on his mind. Like you, I can tell exactly what you're thinking right now."

"That's really great," replied the buyer, "so why don't you go there?"

672.63

Someone asked Salesman Sam for the secret of his success. "If I don't strike oil within five minutes," said Sam, "I quit boring."

672.64

One of the big manufacturers of plaids and tartans in Edinburgh received word that its traveling salesman had expired suddenly in a Liverpool hotel. The manager in Edinburgh wired collect: "Return samples by freight and search his pants for orders."

672.65

I saw a cartoon recently showing a bewildered shopper examining an egg-shaped contraption with a big hole in the middle of it.

The salesman explains: "It's electric. You just stick your head in it, and it shaves you, brushes your teeth, massages your face, combs your hair, and sends you on your way with a cheery recorded word of encouragement."

672.66

Two purchasing agents met at a local bar after the day's work was finished. "Say," asked one of them, "did you ever get in touch with the supplier I suggested?"

"Oh yes," replied the other. "They sent one of their salesmen over and he told me they had just the product I was trying to find."

"Did you tell him I suggested you call them?"

"I did."

"That's good. What did he say?"

"Well, he thought about it for a couple of minutes, and then he asked me to pay in advance."

672.67

The secretary was trying desperately to finish a letter, but that did not deter the story-telling salesman in the slightest. Finally she looked up and said, "Have you ever had a group picture taken of yourself?"

672.68

The art of showmanship is to give the public what it wants just before it knows what it wants.

672.69

The fast-talking salesman could never quite get by the secretary to an important executive. Finally, in desperation, he told her: "You're a nice kid and I want to do something for you. Go down to the jeweler's and get yourself a diamond wristwatch—don't take one worth less than a thousand dollars—and charge it to me."

"Gosh," cooed the secretary, "you're wonderful. Tell me, how can I get in touch with you to express my thanks."

"Just call me at 20-667-0932," he said.

"Is that your home or your business?" she asked.

"It's the candy store downstairs. But don't worry. They always call me."

672.70

Promoter—A man who will provide the galaxy if you provide the rocket ships.

672.71

The sales manager received a telegram from his newest cub salesman: "Must have a salary increase at once," it read, "or count me out."

The manager went to the files and pulled out the salesman's rather dismal sales record. After looking it over, he fired off the following reply: "One, Two, Three, Four, Five, Six, Seven, Eight, Nine, Ten."

672.72

"What a great day I had," said the first salesman. "Made a lot of friends for the company."

"Yeah," said the second salesman, "I didn't sell anything either."

672.73

A good salesman makes you think you've wanted something all your life—even if you never heard of it before!

672.74

"You've got to know how to merchandise if you want to get ahead," the executive told the bootblack.

The next day the boy set off a flood of business with this sign: "One shoe shined FREE."

672.75

Manager to cub salesman, "How come? You claim to be our best salesman, and you can't talk me into giving you a raise."

672.76

A salesman in Woodbridge, Va., said he could sell anything. He then was asked if he could sell elephants. He answered, "Sure, if I can get 'em financed at two dollars down and a dollar a week."

672.77

Yes, he was a super salesman. He sold two milking machines to a farmer with only one cow, and then took the cow as a down payment.

672.78

The sales manager stormed into the company president's office. "That new salesman you hired is absolutely insufferable!" he shouted. "He's offensive and positively insulting! Just now, when I was trying to correct him on his approach, he told me to go soak my head in a bucket. And when I threatened to tell you about it, he said you could take a running jump in the lake!"

"That's too bad," replied the president. "I was sure he would make a good salesman."

"He's a good enough salesman, all right," said the sales manager. "As a matter of fact, he's already sold his entire quota for the month in just the first week."

"In that case," said the president, "maybe I could use a little more exericse, and I'm sure the janitor would be happy to let you borrow one of his pails."

672.79

A salesman finally got an important buyer on the phone and said to him, "I've been trying all week to see you. May I have an appointment?"

"Make a date with my secretary," said the buyer.

"I did, and she's a cute girl," said the salesman, "but I still want to see you."

SCIENCE
SCIENTIST

680.50

The late Albert Einstein, known throughout the world as an eminent physicist and formulator of the theory of relativity, also took pleasure in playing the violin. Once he was playing for an intimate gathering when he noticed the well-known comic dramatist, Ferenc Molnar, was laughing. He stopped playing and asked, "Why do you laugh when I play? Do I ever laugh at your plays?"

680.51

Two moon men watched the astronauts collecting rocks, and one said to the other, "Well, there goes the garden."

680.52

Einstein once commented about a book 100 German scientists had written to disprove his theory of relativity by saying, "If I had been wrong, one professor would have been enough."

680.53

When Thomas Edison was inventing the electric light, he spent years and years trying to find the right kinds of filaments, the right gas, the proper type of container. Finally one day about 2 a.m., he made the thing glow. He ran out of his barn-laboratory, into the house, up three flights of stairs to his wife's bedroom, and said, "Darling, look!"

She woke up, rolled over and said, "Will you shut that light off and come to bed?"

SECRETARY

688.50

A man asked to see the captain of police. The new secretary replied politely, "He's not in. Would you care to leave your fingerprints?"

688.51

Secretary Jane made a habit of coming in late. Her boss, unable to contain himself, remarked one morning as Jane strolled in at 9:45, "You should have been here at nine!"

"Why," answered Jane, "something happen?"

688.52

"I don't know how you do it," said the office manager to his new stenographer. "You've only been here two weeks and you're already a month behind."

688.53

The two secretaries were huddled around the water cooler. "How is your boss on dictation?" asked one.

"He's okay, I guess," replied the other, "but I sure have to take a lot for grunted."

688.54

The president of a large corporation faced his executive force with a stern look on his face and said, "I am going to put it to you squarely, men. My secretary has been going out with one of you, and I want to know which one." There was a look of shock and embarrassment on the faces of every man in the room with the exception of one art director. "Do you mean to tell me you're the only man here who has not been out with her?" the boss asked.

"I am very proud to say that my association with your secretary has been one of a purely business nature and nothing more," replied the young man.

"You're just the man I'm looking for, then," said the boss. "Get right out there and fire her!"

SERVICE
SERVANTS WAITERS WAITRESSES

696.30

Myron Cohen says he knows a waiter who was struck by a horrible cramp in his restaurant and rushed to the hospital. He lay in near total agony, and screamed to a passing doctor, "Doc, you gotta help me! You gotta save my life!"

To which the doctor replied, "Sorry, this isn't my table."

696.31

I hired a hippie maid ... she comes in once a week and dirties up.

696.32

A man said to a waiter, "What's our offense? We've been on bread and water for the past two hours."

696.33

At a service station on a road outside Las Vegas, a sign says: Free Aspirins And Tender Sympathy.

696.34

"Waiter, just how long have you been working here?" demanded the irate customer.

"About two weeks," replied the waiter.

"Oh, I see," said the customer. "Well, in that case, you couldn't have been the one who took my order."

696.35

"Waiter, I ordered lobster salad and there is absolutely no lobster in it."

"That's no surprise. Don't expect too much from our cottage cheese, either."

696.36

Chambermaid (after guest had been ringing for a half hour): "Did you ring, sir?"

Patron: "No, I was only tolling. I thought you had passed away."

696.37

Posted at the exit of a Manhattan self-service auto garage: We use the honor system. Deposit money in slot. Your license number is recorded.

696.38

Two New York motorists were traveling down South and decided to have a cup of coffee in a truck stop. When the waiter came over, one ordered coffee with a little cream and heavy on the sugar. The other took a look around and said, "I'll take mine black, but make sure it's in a clean cup."

Shortly the waiter returned. "Which one," he asked, "gets the clean cup?"

696.39

A modern businessman walked into a barber shop, and the barber told him, "Your hair needs cutting badly."

He replied, "No, it doesn't, it needs cutting well. You cut it badly the last time."

696.40

The neighborhood Scrooge walked into the hardware store and pounded on the floor with his cane. "You're nothing but a gyp artist," he shouted. "I came in here 12 years ago to get a faucet washer and you charged me 5 cents for it."

"Well, it fixed that leaking faucet, didn't it?" asked the puzzled manager.

"Fixed it!" stormed the customer. "You ought to see it now! That danged faucet is leaking again!"

696.41

Ya see in the papers last night where a man went 38 days without food? That's ridiculous ... he should have given his order to another waiter.

696.42

A businessman handed the hotel manager a bouquet of flowers and said in a sympathetic voice, "It's for the switchboard operator."

The manager looked pleased. "Thank you, sir. I'm sure she will appreciate the compliment on her fine service."

"Service!" roared the businessman. "I thought she was dead!"

696.43

Noted author Munro Leaf, driving cross-country with his wife, stopped at a small diner near a railroad crossing where four large trucks were parked. "It's shrewd policy to eat at the same place the truck drivers do," he explained to his wife. "They know the territory like the palm of their hand and always eat where the food is best and most reasonable." But the meal the waitress brought them was poor, almost unpalatable. The waitress noticed their disappointment and sympathized with them. She came over to their table and explained in a whisper, "The boss bought those trucks from a junk dealer and parked them out front. They were cheaper than a neon sign and attract a lot more customers."

SLEEP
DREAMS

706.40

An Ozark native, aged 80 or thereabouts, ambled into a doctor's office in Crane, Missouri, and announced, "Doc, I seem to have picked up a first-class case of insomnia somewhere. I keep wakin' up every few days."

706.41

Next to a beautiful woman, sleep is the greatest thing in the world.

706.42

A man was slightly peeved when a neighbor phoned at four in the morning to say that his dog's barking was keeping the neighborhood awake. At four the next morning, he called the neighbor and said, "I don't have a dog."

706.43

Last night I dreamed of noble things and erected vast empires in my mind. Today I caught the 7:05 to work and acted just as though I'd done nothing extraordinary.

706.44

There is one protest sign understood the world over: the stifled yawn.

706.45

Patient: "Doctor, I'm having dreams in which I see talking mice, and talking crickets, and talking dogs, and talking ducks. What am I having?"
Psychiatrist: "A Disney spell."

706.46

A man and his wife were fast asleep, but the wife was dreaming that she was in another's bedroom. Then she dreamed that she saw her husband coming into the room. She screamed, "My husband!"

Her husband heard her scream and jumped out the window.

706.47

Patient: "Doc, is it true that sleeping outdoors will cure insomnia?"

Doctor: "As well as sleeping indoors."

706.48

Let's have some quiet in here, please . . . my foot is asleep.

706.49

When it comes to protecting us, the National Warning Center never sleeps. And now that I know how efficient they are, I'm not sleeping too good either!

706.50

"So what if your husband does snore?" said the doctor. "Lots of husbands snore."

"Yes," sighed the baggy-eyed wife, "but George is a ventriloquist, and he snores on both sides of me at once."

SPEAKING
TALKING

712.30

Noted journalist Heywood Broun was listening with disbelief to a speaker at a political rally who was giving his version of the facts.

"How can he do this?" whispered a fellow writer. "He's murdering the truth."

Broun disagreed. "He'll never get close enough to it to do it bodily harm," he said.

712.31

A veteran Broadway actor, getting on in years, was finding it more difficult to get the choice parts that had once easily come his way. His agent suggested he go on a lecture tour. The thespian eagerly accepted and agreed to speak before a Midwestern city's little-theater group. Arriving there to find a sparse audience, the actor reluctantly rose to speak: "Ladies and gentlemen, I agreed to speak before this group only because your committee assured me a vast audience would be present. As I look out into this barren hall with all its empty seats, I realize that what I have instead is a half-vast audience."

712.32

"I've never heard anyone talk faster than Eddie in my whole life," a man said.

"Why shouldn't he?" said a friend. "His father was a tobacco auctioneer and his mother was a woman."

712.33

The great Benjamin Disraeli once observed a deaf member of Parliament listening to a dreary, dull speech with the aid of an ear trumpet. Disraeli lamented, "What a wanton waste of the mercies of God's providence."

712.34

Edward R. Murrow, the commentator, was attending an advertising banquet in New York, and the man who was to introduce the speaker droned on for much longer than he should have. When a voice from the rear shouted, "I can't hear a thing," Murrow quickly said, "I'd like to change places with you."

712.35

A man phoned a doctor of my acquaintance not long ago and said, "Doc, my wife dislocated her jaw. If you're out this way in a month or so, would you mind stopping in and taking a look at her?"

712.36

President Calvin Coolidge had a reputation for being a man of few words. One day a woman came up to him and said, "Mr. President, I made a bet that I could make you say three words."

Silent Cal replied, "You lose."

712.37

A reporter went up to a senator after a political speech and said, "Excuse me, Senator, but there were a couple of things I didn't quite understand in your speech today."

"No doubt," said the legislator. "Those are the things I refer to in a confident, offhanded way to avoid revealing the fact that I can't figure them out either."

712.38

A great actor was walking in New York one day when he saw a famous snob coming. He tried to avoid a meeting, but the man yelled out, "Hello. You are absolutely the only person I've met so far today that is worth talking to."

The actor replied, "Really? Then you are so much more fortunate than I."

712.39

A famous actor was scheduled to give a speech on a program where he was preceded by several other speakers. When the program finally dragged around to him, the master of ceremonies said, "And now, Mr. —— will give his address."

Whereupon the actor rose and said, "My address is the Lamb's Club," and returned to his seat.

712.40

A candidate was making a speech in the town hall when a man in the back jumped up and shouted, "Liar!" The candidate quickly said, "If the gentleman would give his name instead of his occupation, I'd be glad to meet him."

712.41

If a thing goes without saying, then let it.

712.42

Public speaking is like drinking. A few men can do it in moderation, but the majority don't know when to stop.

712.43

Recipes for the best speeches should always include shortening.

712.44

Clarence Darrow, the famous lawyer, gave a lecture at a women's club meeting. Afterward the club president approached him and said enthusiastically, "What a wonderful talk, Mr. Darrow. What can we ever do to show our gratitude and appreciation?"

"My dear lady," replied Darrow, "ever since the Phoenicians invented money, there has only been one answer to that question."

712.45

"They say your wife is outspoken."

"By whom?"

712.46

The last day of the sales convention was over, and the sales manager and his wife were at home relaxing before preparing for bed. "What did you think of my speech tonight," asked the sales manager.

"Well, dear," replied his wife, "you got off one thing that made me very proud."

"What was that?" he asked.

"The stage."

712.47

Adlai Stevenson rarely needled other politicians, but one fellow from California had gotten the Illinois senator's goat. Stevenson remarked about the man, "He is the only man I know who could chop down a giant sequoia and stand on the stump and deliver a speech on conservation."

SPORTS

718.15

Two business partners were playing a round of golf one day. On the third tee, one said to the other, "Wait, I think I forgot to take the cash box."

His friend responded, "So what? We're both here, aren't we?"

718.16

An avid golfer married a girl whose passion was attending auctions. They both talked in their sleep. He'd say, "Fore," and she'd say, "Four and a quarter."

718.17

A golfer sliced his drive into the rough. After hunting for quite a while, he finally located the ball near a clump of bushes. Just as he was about to attempt to hit the ball, he heard a voice from inside the clump of bushes.

"Pssst. Do you have any paper out there?"

"No," replied the golfer, "I don't," and started to hit the ball again.

"Psssst," said the voice again. "Do you have any paper in your pockets?"

He was just about to hit the ball when he heard the voice again.

"Well, do you have five ones for a five?"

718.18

A funeral procession was passing a golf course. A man just about to make a putt stopped, removed his hat, and stood in silence until all the cars had passed.

His partner then remarked, "That was a nice gesture, Fred."

Fred responded: "It was the least I could do. We would have been married 31 years next week."

718.19

Two little old ladies inadvertently turned on TV to a professional football game on Sunday afternoon. They watched the teams battle to a scoreless first half. Then, after halftime as the teams were lining up for the kickoff, one of the ladies said, "Let's change it. This is where we came in."

718.20

Famous Notre Dame football coach Frank Leahy decided one day that things were getting a little out of hand with his "lads," so he decided to give a little speech.

"Men," he began, "we're going to return to fundamentals." Picking up a ball he said, "This is a football."

"Wait a minute, coach," said one of his linemen, "not so fast."

718.21

Girl: "What position do you play on the basketball team this season?"

Benchwarmer: "Oh, sort of crouched and bent over."

718.22

Full of confidence, Mr. Blowhard looked down the fairway and casually told his caddy: "This should be good for a long drive and a putt." With that, he took a mighty swing, hit the sod, and the ball rolled only a few feet.

"Boy," said the caddy, "this is going to be one hell of a putt."

718.23

"You have been staring over my shoulder for the past four hours. Why don't you try it yourself?" suggested the fisherman.

"I couldn't," replied his audience. "I don't have the patience."

718.24

I tried to get an appointment with my dentist yesterday afternoon, but he said he couldn't see me because he had 18 cavities to fill. An hour later I saw him at the golf course.

718.25

Two women approached the golf pro. "Do you wish to learn to play, madam?" the pro asked one of them.

"Oh, no," she answered. "It's my friend who wants to learn. I learned yesterday."

718.26

A caddy is one of those little things that count, the worse the better.

718.27

Harry Ruby tells about the prize-fight manager whose inexperienced new middleweight was taking an unmerciful trimming in his first professional bout. Finally the manager propped up his unhappy charge and told him, "I don't care if it's bad luck or not—but this is the ninth round coming up, and, kid, you've got a no-hitter going!"

718.28

A pair of duffers were thrashing about the course. On the fourth hole, one turned to his friend who was keeping score.

"How many did you take on that one?" he asked.

"Ten," replied his companion.

"It was my hole," said the first one. "I only took nine."

After the next hole, the first duffer asked the same question.

"No, you don't," said his friend, "this is my turn to ask first."

718.29

The caddy burst out laughing every time the duffer took a swing. Finally, the duffer could take it no longer. "Laugh one more time," he cautioned, "and I'll hit you over the head with the club."

"Yeah," sneered the caddy, "and you'll probably use the wrong one."

718.30

A Connecticut couple decided to drive up to Boston to see a ball game at Fenway Park. They ran into all sorts of traffic, and when they arrived it was the seventh inning. And the score was 0-0. "That's good," said the wife, "at least we didn't miss anything."

718.31

Trying to alibi after losing a fight, a boxer told his manager: "Boy, did I have that guy worried in the third round."

"You sure did, he thought he'd killed you."

718.32

The late Vince Lombardi was the absolute ruler of the Green Bay Packers. Once, so the story goes, he returned late from a wintry practice session, and crawled into bed.

"God, your feet are cold," exclaimed his wife.

He replied, "You may call me Vincent, my dear."

718.33

A hysterical golfer raced into the clubhouse and said he had just killed his wife. "I didn't know she was behind me and the club hit her right in the head."

"What were you swinging?"

"A number 3 wood."

"Yeah. That one always gives me trouble, too."

718.34

A husband telephoned his wife from the office on Friday afternoon, and said he was going fishing during the weekend and asked her to pack a bag for him.

"Be sure to pack my blue silk pajamas because after a day of fishing, I like to shower and shave and lounge around. It relaxes me better than anything else," he explained.

He returned from his fishing trip, told several anecdotes about his fishing experience and then reproached her:

"Why didn't you pack my blue silk pajamas like I asked you to?"

"I did," she said. "I put them in your tackle box."

718.35

Eddie's deer hunting trip hadn't been doing too well. So one day he went out to a spot where five trails crossed right near a water hole. He quickly hid in the bushes. Then, suddenly, an 11-point buck appeared. Eddie sprang from his sitting position and took three quick shots.

By the time he had the cork back in the bottle, the deer was gone.

718.36

Two boxing managers were discussing the upcoming fight. "Muggsy, my man nails your man with a right cross in the second round and he hits it for the full 10. Got it?"

"Make it the ninth round," said the other, "we don't want to cheat the public."

718.37

"That's a pretty bad slice," said the policeman to the golfer. "It curved right off the course and broke the patrol car window. What are you going to do about it?"

The golfer replied, "Well, the first thing I'm going to do is move my right hand further around the club."

718.38

Scalper—A man who enables you to see one baseball game for the price of the entire World Series.

718.39

A polo expert explained the difference between polo and other games to a sports writer. "With athletes in other games," he noted, "the first thing that usually gives out is the legs. In polo, it's the money."

718.40

A golfer was having an awful day on the public links. Finally, on the eleventh green, he blew a six-inch putt. That did it. He cursed up a storm, threw the ball as far as he could and then broke every club in his bag. Then he turned to his caddie and said, "I've got to quit."

"Quit golf?" asked the caddie.

"No, the priesthood," said the linksman.

718.41

After selling him a huge order, the salesman asked McGee if he'd join him for a round of golf. McGee agreed and, as the two headed for the first hole, expressed his complete lack of skill.

"I confess," he said. "I have only played once before."

"That's funny," said the salesman, "I only played twice —before I hurt my back and broke my arm."

"I'll tell you," said McGee, "so it should be more interesting, how about a tiny little $100 side bet."

The salesman agreed and three hours later McGee was in the club house holding his head in his hands and muttering darkly.

"What happened?" inquired a friend.

"That dirty rat said he couldn't play golf and he came in with a 65!" moaned the salesman.

"What did he beat you by?" asked the friend.

"One up," answered the salesman.

718.42

In Africa, three big-game hunters were resting by their campfire after a hard day in the jungle when one announced, "I'm restless. Think I'll go for a short hike before chow."

The other two didn't fret over his nonappearance for over an hour. Then one glanced at his watch and murmured, "Hmm! Wonder what's eating old Ernest?"

718.43

Two ants lived in an anthill on the first tee of a famous golf course. One day an inept golfer took a swing, missed the ball and lifted a huge chunk of sod far into the air. As the ants watched, he swung again and sent a divot flying which almost struck the ants.

As the duffer prepared to take his third swing, one ant turned to his companion and said, "If we want to get out of this alive, we'd better get on the ball."

718.44

A basketball coach just came up with a terrific idea to get eight-foot players—seven-foot girls!

718.45

If you want to watch a football game in the worst way, take your wife.

718.46

Alumni director to banished Big Ten football coach: "There's a train leaving in an hour. Be under it."

718.47

One of the quickest ways to meet new people is to hit the wrong ball on the golf course.

718.48

Two ball players were walking to the park one morning, and one said to the other, "Say, you didn't do too well with that millionaire's daughter last night."

His friend agreed saying, "No runs, no hits, no heiress."

718.49

A hunter once climbed over a stone wall carrying a loaded and cocked rifle. He was survived by his wife, three children, and a rabbit.

718.50

Angry golfer: "You must be absolutely the worst caddie in the world."

Caddie: "That, sir, would be one remarkable coincidence."

718.51

Said a wife, "Herb had good luck on his hunting trip—he came back alive."

718.52

Ben Hogan, all-time golfing great, was foiled one day when he tried to give a duffer the thrill of a lifetime. Ben and a friend were playing a practice round. They had just holed out on a short three-par hole whose green was partially surrounded by trees and traps when suddenly, out of nowhere, a ball plopped down and trickled within two inches of the cup.

Hogan playfully tapped the ball in and, when a red-faced player came puffing from the direction of the deepest trap, held out his hand and said, "Mister, you're in for the biggest kick you ever got out of golf. Just look in that cup." The player followed directions and then hollered to a partner still out of view, "Hey, Joe, whaddya know! I sank it for a seven!"

718.53

The wife of one of the forwards on the New York Rangers hockey team admitted, "It's really thrilling to be married to a big-time hockey star. Every time he comes home he looks like a different person."

718.54

The Idle Hour Athletic Club was putting on one of its better fixed fights, with the five-to-one favorite bribed in advance to let himself be knocked cold in the eighth round. The underdog, secure in the knowledge that he couldn't lose, let a couple of real punches loose and rattled every tooth in the favorite's head.

"You dirty little double-crosser," hissed that gentleman in a clinch. "Just wait till I get you outside!"

718.55

An ex-baseball pitcher took up a boxing career. By the end of the fourth round of his first fight, he was battered beyond belief. His manager said, "I gotta stop the fight."

The man replied, "Don't you dare. This is my first no-hitter."

718.56

We know of a college that is deemphasizing athletics. They won't give a football player his letter until he knows what letter it is.

718.57

Two golfers were imbibing at the 19th hole and fell into conversation.

"The missus says she is going to leave me if I don't give up playing golf," one concluded.

"Gosh, that's terrible," replied his companion.

"Yeah, I know. I'm going to miss her, too."

718.58

A game hunter recounted his experience with a wounded lion. "As he charged me at full speed, I jumped for an overhanging branch that was at least 15 feet over my head."

"Did you make it?" asked the listener.

"No, I missed it on my way up," the hunter explained, "but managed to grab it on my way back down."

718.59

The fight was going rather badly for a boxer, so between rounds his manager said, "Forget he ran off with your wife. Pretend you really hate him."

718.60

Jones must be getting ready for his fishing trip. Today he was buying an enlarging device for his camera.

718.61

"When did that little twirp ever get athlete's foot?"

"When a football player caught him out with his girl."

718.62

St. Peter saw a man trying to enter the Pearly Gates one day. He stopped him and said, "Sorry, but you've told too many lies to get in here."

"Gimme a break," pleaded the man, "you were a fisherman once yourself."

718.63

Three hunters on safari were trapped in a tree by several tigers. One man turned to one of the others and said, "Drat it, Quigley, you're a Princeton man. Do something about this."

718.64

It was hunting season and the man was in a sporting goods store stocking up on equipment for his annual outing. One item he picked up was a compass, but he was puzzled by the fact that it had a mirror on the back. Finally he cornered a sales clerk and asked, "What's the idea of this combination?"

"Oh, that," replied the clerk. "Well, when you're using this compass, you simply turn it over and look in there. It will tell you immediately who's lost."

718.65

The salesman was idolized by his young son, and in the face of such worship he couldn't help but foster, by word and attitude, his worthiness of the tribute. One day, upon returning from an afternoon at the golf course, the youngster asked his father, "Did you win again today, Daddy?"

"Let's put it this way," replied the fast-thinking father, "your daddy got to hit the ball more times than anyone else."

718.66

Judge: "And how exactly did the trouble start?"
Defendant: "Well, she asked me to play a round, and I didn't know she was a golfer."

718.67

Golfer: "I'm certainly not playing my usual game."
Caddie: "What game is that?"

718.68

Two golfers looked up in time to see an atom bomb demolish the distant city.

"Go ahead and putt," said one. "It'll be a few minutes before the shock wave hits us."

718.69

Freshman football candidate: "I'm a little stiff from bowling."

Coach: "I don't care where you're from. Get out there and play some ball."

718.70

One coach has the final solution, he thinks, for the regulation of big-time college football: one squad for offense, one for defense, and one to attend classes.

718.71

A golfer lost his temper one day and shouted at a friend, "Shut up. If you keep this up, you'll drive me out of my mind."

His friend said casually, "That wouldn't be a drive, that would be a putt."

718.72

A minister glared at one of his parishioners and said, "I understand you went to a ball game Sunday instead of to church."

"That's a lie, Reverend, and I've got a fish to prove it."

718.73

Some brand-new members of a hunting club were coming in from their first day's shooting. Since they were unused to handling guns, the casualty list was formidable. One had his hand in a sling, another was hopping on one foot, a third looked like the drummer boy in the old Revolutionary War picture. "Cheer up, fellows," urged an old member. "Judging by the bulge in your bag, you're not coming back empty-handed, anyhow!"

The one who was carrying the bag answered wearily, "That's our hunting dog!"

718.74

While out hunting, a fellow was amazed to see a beautiful young lady go running by followed by two men in white suits. A third man, carrying a large sandbag, followed some distance behind.

"What the devil's going on?" asked the hunter of the man carrying the sandbag.

"This girl escaped from the asylum and we've got to catch her," explained the puffing attendant.

"I see," said the hunter, "but why the sandbag?"

"Oh," said the man in white. "She escaped yesterday and I caught her. This is my handicap."

718.75

Hunter: "I got three deer and a potfur."
Friend: "What's a potfur?"
Hunter: "To cook the meat in."

718.76

Winding up at the eighteenth hole at the Thunderbird Golf Club in Palm Springs, Danny Thomas handed the caddy $5 and told him to give a dollar to the clubhouse boy. The next time out, he asked the clubhouse boy if he had gotten his dollar. The boy shook his head. "That's funny," Danny said, "I told the caddy to give you a dollar." The clubhouse boy replied, "Mr. Thomas, you might just as well have sent a lettuce leaf by a rabbit."

TAXES

742.40

"I hear the Internal Revenue Service has hired a psychiatrist to do their public relations."

"What is he saying?"

"Something about it not being good to keep too much to yourself."

742.41

In this country of ours, every little toddler, no matter how humble or poor his background, can grow up and become a taxpayer.

742.42

"Let's stop all this nonsense," said the businessman to his accountant. "I want to pay my taxes all in one lump sum."

"But you are permitted to pay them quarterly," the accountant said.

"I know," came the reply, "but my heart can't take it four times a year."

742.43

A businessman who was near death asked that his remains be cremated and the ashes be mailed to the Internal Revenue Service with the following note attached: "Now you have it all."

742.44

The exasperated salesman was called in for an income tax review and questioning by an Internal Revenue Service agent about his deducations. After the session went on for over an hour, he blurted out: "I wish the Government were half as fussy about how *it* spends its money as it is about how *I'm* spending mine!"

742.45

Why does a slight tax increase cost you $200 and a substantial tax cut save you 30 cents?

742.46

Internal Revenue agent: Someone you really have to hand it to.

742.47

Untold wealth—Those funds not listed on the income tax return.

742.48

The way things are now, if I didn't have to pay my taxes, I'd still be broke.

742.49

If these darn taxes get any worse, you won't have to go to the poorhouse ... stay home. Your house is as good as theirs.

742.50

A Texan walked into a bar and asked for the tallest glass in the house. The bartender gave it to him. He then produced an orange from his pocket, and squeezed it in his hand until he had a full glass of juice.

"There," he said, "I'd like to see anyone get that much juice out of an orange!"

A meek little man standing next to him asked for the orange peel and a similar glass. He then produced so much juice from the peel that the glass overflowed.

"Well, I'll be!" said the Texan. "How did you do that?"

"It's fairly easy," said the man. "You see, I'm with the Internal Revenue Service."

742.51

One thing death has over taxes—death doesn't get worse every time the state assembly meets.

742.52

The word "tax" comes from the Latin taxare, which means "to touch sharply." Satis dicit (enough said).

742.53

A Boston traveler described the Eiffel Tower as "the Prudential Building after taxes."

742.54

Hear about the streamlined income tax form? All it says is:
- (A) How much did you earn last year?
- (B) How much is left?
- (C) Send B.

750.50

"My God, I saw your obituary in this morning's paper!"

"I know. I put it there myself. My opera is being produced tonight, and I want a good review."

750.51

Mark Twain's hostess at an opera was talking so much during the performance that no one in the box had been able to enjoy it. When it was over, she said, "Mr. Clemens, I'd like you to be my guest next week, too. They're going to give Tosca then."

"Charmed," said Twain, "I've never heard you in that."

750.52

The theater once held a mirror up to life—now it holds up a keyhole.

750.53

Theater reviewers have provided some of the funniest lines in American humor. One reviewer, after a classical concert, noted that the pianist "played Brahms and lost."

750.54

Some months ago, the author of a Broadway show, which never made it because of financial problems, attended the auditions for a part which required a beautiful young actress to dance wildly in a revealing bikini. Many futile attempts at the role were made by aspiring actresses, but none of them were very impressive until Carol Cady, a lovely performer noted particularly for her shapely legs, did her dance. The author, turning to the producer, said, "That's the best darned bit of writing I've ever done!"

750.55

One of those new Broadway shows closed after a one-week run recently. They lost $2.37 on costumes alone.

750.56

A reviewer once said that a famous actress "ran the gamut of emotion from A to B."

750.57

A Boston reviewer began a play review by saying that the only action he had been able to perceive "was that of the paint drying on the backdrop."

750.58

A famous actress's performance of Cleopatra did not sit well with a reviewer, who said the actress "sailed down the Nile and sank."

750.59

A young writer presented his first play to a producer and later called to ask what he thought of it. "It's a great play," said the producer, "it's a very fresh and original approach and the writing is superb."

"Then you'll buy it?"

"Oh, no," replied the producer. "I can't take a chance on something that's never been done before."

TIME
TIMING, CLOCKS, etc.

756.40

Our population increases at the rate of one person every 10.5 seconds. We can't control the population but we at least have it timed.

756.41

"Did I hear the clock strike two when you came in?" said the irate wife to her husband.

"Yes, dear, you did. It was trying to strike 10, but I stopped it so it wouldn't wake you."

756.42

The nice thing about gardening is that if you put it off long enough . . . eventually, it will be too late.

756.43

Store manager to salesman coming in half an hour late: "You should have been here at 8."

Salesman: "Why, what happened?"

756.44

May Fate and Time conspire in such a way as to allow all good men to write their own epitaphs.

756.45

You can take the day off, but you can't put it back!

756.46

Expedite: to make a normally slow operation come to a complete standstill.

756.47

I took my boy to the autorama yesterday, and they had a special display of highly unusual motor vehicles ... they even had a (city) bus that ran on time.

756.48

A distracted mother rushed into the doctor's office and exclaimed, "My child swallowed an alarm clock!"

"Does it bother him so far?" asked the doctor.

"Well, it doesn't bother him so much," she said, "but every time I try to wind it, he bites my finger."

756.49

A workman had climbed a steep ladder and was perched precariously on the rim of the city hall clock. He was obviously cleaning the huge dial when a passerby stopped to watch.

"What's wrong?" the passerby asked. "Is something wrong with the clock?"

"It's fine," replied the workman. "I'm just nearsighted."

756.50

Noticing that a nostalgia craze was sweeping the country, the aged antique dealer turned to his wife and said, "You know, Florence, if this keeps up, these could be the good old days."

756.51

The men from the office stopped for a few friendly drinks before starting home. As the time progressed, one salesman was seen to glance more and more frequently at his watch. Finally he got up and started for the door. "What's the matter, Joe?" asked one of the men. "Afraid your wife will give you a hard time if you stay out too late?"

"Not really," replied Joe, "but it never hurts to play safe. I'm just going down to the station to miss the next train home. I'll be right back."

756.52

There's only one trouble with alarm clocks . . . they always go off when you're asleep.

TRAVEL
TRANSPORTATION

762.30

A man was touring Greece, and sent back a postcard to his son with the following inscription: "Dear Son, on the reverse you will see a picture of the rock upon which the Spartans used to throw their defective children. Wish you were here."

762.31

People were happier back in the horse-and-buggy days. They had a stable economy.

762.32

Cross your bridges before you come to them and you have to pay the toll twice.

762.33

The little woman had insisted on bringing every piece of clothing she owned. The couple arrived at the station, and the husband said, "I wish we'd brought your piano."

"Knock that off," came the curt reply.

"No, I mean it. I left the tickets on it."

762.34

The trouble with modern transportation is that there is no longer any such thing as a distant relative.

762.35

A guy from Brooklyn took his wife to Newark for a flight to Detroit. After fighting the traffic to get home, he entered the house and saw a telegram under the door. It read, "Arrived safely, love, Marrianne."

762.36

We just got back from out West ... those western gals are just wonderful ... you can always tell them from the eastern gals. The eastern gals don't chew tobacco!

762.37

In Alaska in the thirties, a sweet if not too bright young thing was walking near Juneau with a pilot when a plane flew overhead.

"That's a mail plane," he reported.

She answered, "How can you tell at that distance?"

762.38

With mass transit to the moon almost a reality, this one is bound to come up. A young man approached an airline ticket office and asked for a ticket to the moon.

"Sorry," said the counterman, "all flights are canceled."

"Bad weather?" asked the man.

"No, the moon is full right now."

762.39

Air traffic is getting as bad as automobile traffic. Last month I was in a holding pattern over New York so long that the plane became obsolete.

762.40

Two little old ladies in tennis shoes boarded a plane for their first flight. One of them approached the pilot and said: "Now, young man, be sure and don't fly faster than sound. We want to talk."

762.41

I won't say the ship on which I just took a Caribbean cruise was old, but it was insured against fire, theft, and falling off the end of the world.

762.42

Ah, the jet age ... breakfast in Paris ... lunch in Hong Kong ... dinner in London ... baggage in Seattle.

762.43

The elegantly dressed lady entered the city bus and deposited 20 cents in the fare box and sat down.

"Lady," said the driver, "the fare is 30 cents."

"Oh, I beg your pardon," said the lady in somewhat snobbish tones. "I haven't been on a bus for years. You know, normally I have a chauffeured car to drive me."

"Gee," said the bus driver, "you don't know how much we've missed you."

762.44

Aircraft hijackings are getting so frequent these days that couples going on honeymoons to Florida are pelted with Spanish rice.

762.45

The takeoff on my daughter's first plane trip was pretty smooth, so I asked her, "Dear, what do you think of your first plane trip?"

She said: "Great, Daddy, but when do we start getting smaller?"

762.46

It was a beautiful spring morning and four high school boys decided to skip classes. Arriving after lunch, they explained to the teacher that their car had a flat tire along the way.

To their relief, the teacher smiled understandingly and said:

"You boys missed a test this morning. Please take seats apart from one another and get out your paper and pencil."

When the boys were seated, she continued, "For your test, just answer this one question, 'Which tire was flat'?"

762.47

"I'm going to fly this thing right to the sun," said the rather specious pilot.

"You jerk. The sun is much too hot," said a friend.

"I'm going to go at night," he replied.

762.48

I won't say it was a small airline, but we dusted crops on the way here.

762.49

Two men ran after the same cab on a busy cross-town street. After a short discussion, one of them returned to his wife at the curb.

"Why did you let him have the cab?" she demanded. "We were really here first."

"Well, you see," replied her husband, "he was late for his karate class."

762.50

Salesman to airline clerk: "How can anything that goes 800 miles an hour be late?"

762.51

Because her territory scored the highest points in an incentive contest, the office secretary was included on an incentive trip aboard a luxury liner. Second day out the ship ran into a storm, and she was overcome with seasickness as she was undressing in her cabin.

In a panic, she rushed into the corridor and hurried for the bathroom. It wasn't until she collided with an elderly gentleman, a dealer from Iowa who was equally miserable, that she realized that she didn't have a stitch of clothes on. Horrified, she let out a shriek.

The suffering dealer looked at her wanly. "Don't let it bother you, miss," he groaned, "I'll never live to tell anybody."

762.52

A minister who was beginning to get a little apprehensive about air travel went to see a statistician one day.

"Can you tell me," he asked, "What the odds are on my boarding an aircraft that has a bomb hidden on it?"

The man checked all the available data and then told him, "The odds against your getting on a plane with a bomb hidden on it are a million to one."

"Those are good odds, but I don't know if they are good enough. I travel quite a bit."

"Well," he answered, "if you really want to be safe, take a bomb with you. The odds are a billion to one against boarding an aircraft with two bombs on it."

762.53

One salesman to another: "Yes, I took my wife to Las Vegas with me. You know how it is when you take a trip. You always pack something you don't need."

762.54

Two Americans met on the Champs Elysee on their first visit to Paris. "This sightseeing sure takes a lot of time," grumbled one. "I've been here nearly four days and I still haven't been to the Louvre."

Suggested the other, "Maybe it's the water."

762.55

Man at airline ticket counter: "I'll take two chances on your next flight to Miami."

762.56

The lady tourist was admiring the Indian's necklace. "What are those things?" she asked.

"Alligators' teeth," he replied.

After recovering her composure she said, "Well, I suppose that they hold the same meaning for you as pearls do for us."

"Not quite," he answered. "Anybody can open an oyster."

TRUTH
TRUTH-TELLING

770.50

A friend of mine said he lived in an outlying village in Vermont. He said the people there could outlie anyone else in the world.

770.51

A father was spanking his seven-year-old son for telling a whopper.

"I never told lies when I was your age, son," he said.

"Gee, Dad, how old were you when you started?" asked the lad.

770.52

Women are to blame for most of the lying done by men. They insist on asking questions.

770.53

Returning home very late one night, a man alibied that he had been out with his business manager.

"That's nice," said his wife. "He's waiting for you in the living room."

"Well," snorted the man, "who you gonna believe—me or your eyes?"

VACATION

780.50

A timid employee approached his tyrannical boss and asked for a two-week vacation.

"Two weeks," screamed the boss, "you're trying to subvert this organization. Why in the world do you want to take two weeks off?"

"Because," said the man, "I'd like to have the honor of accompanying my wife on her honeymoon."

780.51

Two women were discussing vacations. One said, "Last year, it was Cannes, and my husband had a wild time. The year before that it was Majorca, and he went bananas. This year I think I'd better go with him."

780.52

If you want to spend your vacation at a faraway place with a strange sounding name and very few other people, let your wife read the road map.

780.53

A psychiatrist received a note from a patient who was vacationing in the Virgin Islands. It read, "Having a ball. Wish you were here to tell me why."

780.54

"How did you get that big black smudge on your nose?" Henry asked.

"Oh," said Bill, "I took my wife to the train station and saw her off on a three-month vacation."

"Yeah, but what about the smudge?"

"As soon as she got on board, I ran up and kissed the engine."

780.55

If you did all the things you really *should* do before you go on vacation, it would be over before you started.

780.56

The way things are being speeded up, it won't be long before a person can take 2 weeks' vacation in 4 days.

VISION
SEEING   EYEGLASSES

788.50

I never look at another woman: I'm too faithful ... I'm too honest ... I'm too nearsighted!

788.51

"When I go to bed at night I see little black squares and red circles."

"Have you ever seen a psychiatrist?"

"No, just little black squares and red circles."

788.52

A woman was pulled over for speeding, and the cop asked to see her license. It was a restrictive license, which said that she must wear glasses at all times when driving. The officer, seeing that she was barefaced, asked, "Where are your glasses?"

She said, "But, officer, I have contacts."

"I don't care who you know, I'm going to give you a ticket anyway."

788.53

"Driving used to be a snap," said the veteran salesman to his cohorts at the office. "There was no traffic problem to worry about, no crazy drivers, nobody cutting in in front of you. But now it's terrible. Cars come at you from every direction."

"I don't agree with you," commented one of the other salesmen. "Ever since I've been driving there have always been a bunch of nitwits on the road. When did you notice a change?"

"Oh, about two weeks ago when I got my new eyeglasses," was the reply.

788.54

Then there is the one about the eager optician who fell into the lens-grinding machine and made a spectacle of himself.

788.55

It's not true that men seldom make passes at girls who wear glasses. It all depends on their frames.

788.56

I'll have to admit my glasses have helped me—since I started wearing them, I haven't had a single black eye.

WEALTH

798.50

A Texas oil man was making out his will. He said to his lawyer, "And to my son I leave four million dollars—and he's lucky I didn't cut him off entirely."

798.51

My uncle's so rich he has a private chauffeur just to drive him crazy.

798.52

"That poor man behind bars was ruined by untold wealth."
"How's that?"
"He didn't tell the IRS about it."

798.53

A rather snobbish rich woman constantly flaunted her wealth. One day as she sat in her custom Rolls limousine with her small daughter comfortably beside her wearing a miniature copy of the mother's mink coat, the chauffeur was about to close the door. Just then a neighbor passed by and gushed, "Oh, what a lovely child. Can she walk?"
"Thank God, she doesn't have to," said the snooty one.

798.54

The newly rich tycoon promptly did the expected thing and bought himself an immense house, complete with servants and all the rest of the accouterments of wealth and elegance.
One evening, as he and his wife were finishing dinner, his wife asked, "Well, dear, shall we have our after-dinner coffee in the library?"
"Oh, I don't know," he replied. "It's such a bother. And besides, it's too late. The library closes at six-thirty."

798.55

A very wealthy man's relatives were gathered, after his death, for the reading of the will. The lawyer began: "Being of sound mind, I spent it all . . ."

798.56

Don't worry about a humble office. A man visited John D. Rockefeller once and twitted the millionaire about the sparse furnishings in his office.

"Don't you want to impress people?" said the guest.

"Whom do I want to impress?" asked Rockefeller.

798.57

My uncle is loaded! He's so rich, he just bought his dog a boy to play with.

WEATHER
SEASONS   TEMPERATURE   CLIMATE

804.50
Postcard to Weather Bureau: "Sirs: I thought you would be interested in knowing that I have just shoveled three feet of partly cloudy from my front steps."

804.51
A man who lived on the Michigan-Indiana border wondered for years which state he actually lived in. Finally he hired a surveyor.

"You definitely live in Indiana," said the surveyor.

"Great," said the man, "no more of those blustery Michigan winters."

804.52
Sunburn—Getting what you basked for.

804.53
I'm really worried. Either we've had an exceptionally cold winter or my wife is carrying on with the oil man.

804.54
Building superintendent: A man known by the temperature he keeps.

804.55
Two Boston ladies were vacationing in Los Angeles when one remarked: "Lord, it never gets this hot back home."

"Of course not," said the other. "You have to remember that we're 3,000 miles from the ocean."

804.56

I solved my perspiration problem for only $233! I moved to Alaska.

804.57

Sunbather: A fry in the ointment.

804.58

Ah . . . Now that spring is here, I'm a real fresh-air fiend. Every morning, I jump out of bed at 5 a.m. . . . run to the window . . . take a deep breath of clean fresh air . . . and then jump back in bed.

804.59

And then there was the woman who was shopping for thermometers, and finally settled upon a Fahrenheit because she knew it was a good brand.

804.60

This past summer brought out all the old stories about weather, like the one attributed to a Vermonter to whom a visitor said, "Hear you had a fine summer in Vermont." The alleged reply, "Dunno, I musta been away that day."

804.61

One of the office girls had just received an engagement ring but to her bitter disappointment no one noticed. Finally, out of desperation, she remarked in loud, clear tones: "My, it's hot in here. Think I'll take off my diamond."

WEIGHT
WEIGHT REDUCING

806.40

"For years, I've been weighing myself on those pay scales that spit out a little card. When I started I weighed 150, now I weigh 195."

"How is it that you gained so much?"

"My pockets are full of those little cards."

806.41

My wife is kinda thin ... last week we went to the beach, and a dog tried to bury her!

806.42

Doctor to obese patient: "You may eat anything you like. Here is a list of what you will like."

806.43

This guy is so thin that he looks like an advance man for a famine.

806.44

If you think old soldiers just fade away, just try to get into your old army uniform.

806.45

Writers George Bernard Shaw and Gilbert K. Chesterton were known for their slim and rotund figures, respectively. Chesterton once said to Shaw, "To look at you, Shaw, a person would think there was a famine in England."

To which Shaw replied, "Yes, and to look at you, he'd think you were the cause of it."

806.46

My wife doesn't like the taste of her reducing pills. So she crunches them up and mixes them with the nuts on her hot fudge sundaes.

806.47

A large woman came up to a policeman and said, "Could you see me across the street?"

The policeman replied, "Lady, I could see you a mile away."

806.48

I wouldn't say my wife is fat, but every morning she has to swing back and forth to get out of bed and rocks herself back to sleep.

806.49

"I am not really overweight," said the wife hotly to her husband, who had suggested that she shed a few pounds. "It's just that according to this chart I should be seven inches taller."

806.50

My brother-in-law is extremely sensitive about being overweight, but I have to rib him about it. The only exercise he gets is when his flesh crawls.

WOMEN

814.40

Woman driver: A person who drives the same way a man does, only she gets blamed for it.

814.41

The defendant admitted he hadn't spoken to his wife in three years. "Just what is your explanation for this?" demanded the judge. "Why haven't you spoken to your wife for three years?"

"Well, your honor," replied the fellow, "I didn't want to interrupt her."

814.42

Women who look for sugar daddies wind up with gray blades.

814.43

To a woman there are two kinds of secrets: One is not worth keeping and the other is too good to keep.

814.44

The adaptability of the human animal never fails to amuse us: We've just heard about the girl who was picked up so often she began to grow handles.

814.45

A woman had just left the hairdressers, and ran into a friend on the street.

"Elaine, what did you do to your hair? It looks like a wig," said the friend.

"It is a wig," was the reply.

"My gracious," she said, "I never would have known it."

814.46

A mixed group was discussing beauty and women. "I think the most fascinating thing about a woman is her mouth," said one fellow.

"I can't agree," said another, "I think it's her hair."

"You're both wrong," said a third. "It's her eyes."

A lady in the party excused herself and said, "I'm getting out of here before one of you guys tells the truth."

814.47

All this nonsense about equality bores me. Women were meant to be loved, not to be understood.

814.48

The Silent Majority is three people in an elevator with Jane Fonda and Martha Mitchell.

814.49

The trouble with life is that there are so many delightful women—and so little time.

814.50

A girl reporter, sent to interview the famous painter Pablo Picasso, asked him recently why mature men generally look younger than mature women. Picasso thought for a minute, then quickly explained, "It's because a woman of 40 is usually 50."

814.51

When a noted psychologist finished his address at a local women's club, one of the women approached him and said, "Isn't it true, doctor, that a woman is the best judge of a woman?"

"Not only the best judge," said the psychologist. "The best executioner."

814.52

A girl's first duty is to her hairdresser. Her second duty hasn't yet been discovered.

814.53

My daughter takes after her mother. The other day I asked, "Where are the Azores?"

She said, "If you just put things away, you'll be able to find them."

814.54

I've noticed an interesting thing about women—the more they worry, the blonder they get!

814.55

If some men hear a secret, it goes in one ear and out the other. When some women hear it, however, it goes in both ears and out their mouths.

814.56

I admire women for their beauty, respect them for their intelligence, adore them for their charm, and love them because I can't help it.

814.57

A distinguished-looking gentleman decided to surprise his wife with a new pair of stockings, so he went to a women's shop where a sale was in progress. After waiting for about an hour on the periphery of a howling mob of women, he blasted in like a fullback.

"Can't you act like a gentleman?" shrieked one hysterical woman.

"Madam," he replied, "I have been acting like a gentleman for the past hour. Now I'm going to act like a lady."

814.58
Women, generally speaking . . . are generally speaking.

814.59
If you want your wife to listen attentively to what you say, address your remarks to another woman.

814.60
I really don't know much about girls . . . just what I've been able to pick up.

814.61
The average woman spends 90% of her time sitting . . . as figures will plainly show.

WRITING
WRITERS

822.50

I just bought a gassy new type fountain pen ... you fill it with water, and it writes under ink.

822.51

James Thurber once met a lady at a cocktail party who told him his books were even funnier in French. "Ah, yes," Thurber said, "I lose something in the original."

822.52

An aspiring poet once sent a poem to Eugene Field which was entitled "Why do I live?" Field immediately wired back: "Because you sent your poem by mail."

822.53

W. C. Fields hated writers. Once he was asked what his favorite fish was and he replied, "A piranha in a writer's bathtub."

822.54

An editor is the man who separates the wheat from the chaff and throws away the wheat.

822.55

William Dean Howells, author, critic and editor, had a reputation for being one of the friendliest men alive. But even Howells couldn't quite stand one particularly conceited author. The man once told Howells, "I get richer and richer, but all the same I think my work is falling off. My new work is not as good as my old."

Summoning his renowned wit, Howells replied, "Nonsense, you're writing as well as you ever did. But your taste is improving."

822.56

An idealistic woman once scolded a writer of popular novels, and told him that nothing he had written would live.

The man told her she was probably right, but said, "When it's a question of me or my work, I always sacrifice the writings."

YOUTH
YOUTHS

824.50

We gotta lick this juvenile delinquency problem ... We gotta figure out ways to keep the kids off the streets ... like building bigger pool halls!

824.51

You can't tell about too much these days. Twenty years ago mothers had their daughters vaccinated in places they thought wouldn't show.

824.52

A baby-sitter is one who eats your food, drinks your beer, watches your TV, breaks your records, and ruins all your furniture ... all for the sum of only $1.00 per hour.

824.53

College senior to his girl: "I'll call you tonight or dial in the attempt."

824.54

Frank is one of the most naïve parents in the world—he still believes his teen-agers are where he told them to be.

824.55

A "now" teen-ager slowly surveyed his older brother and said, "I'll bet you were really conservative when you were my age. I bet you drove a 'warm rod'!"

824.56

The voting age had just been reduced to eighteen, so my son came up to me and said, "It's a good thing you're not running for anything."

824.57

Girl: "My boy friend is a real pacifist. He was the only one at the peace rally who didn't get into a fight."

824.58

Definition of a hippie: He with a she haircut.

824.59

Perhaps our anger at the younger generation is misplaced; Diogenes struck the father when the son swore.

824.60

A young child, somewhat afraid of his first visit to the dentist, looked in awe at a teen-ager dressed in wild psychedelic jeans, an orange cloak, a Robin Hood hat, and sandals. As he left, the youngster asked his mother, "Is that the tooth fairy?"

"There's only one way to make sure you give the best talk you possibly can," said a well-known industrialist when asked for the secret of his success. "Know your subject, plan your speech. This means you must know not only what to say, but how to say it." We all envy the man who can rise to the occasion and talk on the spur of the moment, seemingly with no preparation at all. But there's a reason for this—he actually prepares himself. He knows his subject so thoroughly that he can discuss it at a moment's notice.

SPEECH IMPROVEMENT

Outlining your talk on paper helps you present your ideas in the place they'll be most effective. Only after you see and study your outline can you be fairly certain your talk will accomplish its purpose. You may want to draw up your outline with phrases or sentences that will launch you into each topic. Or perhaps you'd prefer to use key words that will give you your cue. You may want to use large cards or small ones. Whatever you do, make your outline fit your purpose.

The purpose of your talk will dictate what type of outline you'll use. If you talk to instruct, you may want to present your material in chronological order. If you want to convince, the order will be logical. And if your purpose is to praise, you'll probably present your speech in topical form.

Organize Your Outline

After you're through with all your research, jot down the first thought that comes to mind. Before you get that first idea on paper, another will occur to you. Write that down, too. Don't weight its importance. Continue writing down every thought, and soon you'll have one or two dozen ideas you can use. If they seem unimportant or irrelevant, don't worry. Just continue thinking about them. You'll find that small ideas often suggest bigger ideas.

Next, go through your list and evaluate your ideas. Check the ones you think are best, cross out the rest. This will stimulate your thinking and give you clues to other ideas you can use. Once you're sure you have all the ideas you need to accomplish the purpose of your speech, number them in order of importance.

Finally, arrange your ideas in systematic order. *Example*: Assume you've recently been appointed general manager of a factory. After a week or so on your job, you recognize a crucial need for methods improvement. Since you're responsible for your company's production, you want to talk at a meeting with top management. Here's a basic outline you might use:

A. Explain what's wrong with the way things are being done, and why.

B. Strengthen your argument with facts and statistics. Here you discuss your answers to the following questions—
  1. Departmental Layout
     a) Are the machines and work places located so as to keep materials handling to a minimum?
     b) Does the work flow through each department in a reasonably straight line, or does it move back and forth?
     c) Is there adequate storage area?
     d) Are aisles kept open?
     e) What other arrangement of machines could be made? Would it be better? What would it save?
  2. Equipment
     a) How old is it?
     b) Is much time lost due to breakdowns?
     c) Are repair costs too high?
     d) Is equipment being operated at the right speeds?
     e) Are there newer and more efficient machines on the market?
     f) How long would it take to pay for new machines in terms of probable or possible savings?
  3. Operations Analysis
     a) Are these operations necessary?
     b) How much time is lost on the jobs? Why?
     c) What can be done to minimize or eliminate lost time?
     d) Are employees doing their jobs efficiently?
     e) Were they properly instructed?
     f) Are all their work steps necessary?
     g) Is their work being done in the shortest, simplest, and most effective way?

h) Do we know for sure what a fair day's work is on each job?

i) Are we getting it? If not, why not?

4. Material

a) What are the losses due to scrap, spoiled work, and re-operations?

b) What are the specific reasons for these losses?

c) Within whose control are these reasons for the losses?

d) How can these losses be reduced?

e) What's the present status of quality control?

f) Are these standards being met? If not, why not?

g) Is much time lost waiting for materials?

h) If so, exactly how much? Why?

5. Sequence of Operations

a) Are we now using the most efficient sequence of operations?

b) Can any be combined?

c) Can any be done some other way at less cost? If so, how?

6. Materials Handling

a) What does it cost us to handle materials?

b) Is the material handling equipment itself efficient?

Note: Obviously, it's impossible to draw up typical questions which will apply to all types of industry. These questions are intended only as examples of how you can add strength to your talk by citing specific facts and information.

C. Suggest a corrective course of action—a remedy—by proposing specifically what should be done.

D. Make an urgent appeal for definite steps to be taken—by giving your proposal a trial.

Try These Outlines

Here are some flexible outlines you can use. You'll find you can adapt them to your needs in organizing your talk:

1. Give the background or history of a problem.
2. Describe the current condition, rank or standing.
3. Discuss future possibilities.
4. Explain what these possibilities mean, in terms of your listeners' self-interest.
5. Suggest what can be done to correct the problem. Be specific with the facts and figures you use.

Or:

1. Describe resistance shown to new ideas.

2. Explain reasons for resistance to new ideas.
3. Give detailed account of present status of new ideas.
4. Discuss what you're doing to overcome resistance. Give case histories.
5. Describe how your personal investigation points way to overcome resistance. Again, give case histories.
6. Talk about future possibilities of your findings; about urgency of course of action to be taken now.

Or:

1. Discuss new application of an old idea.
2. Describe old and new uses for the idea.
3. Explain how and why your survey (investigation, research, study, or inquiry) has been made.
4. Analyze all the findings shown by survey.
5. Specify how new idea fits current needs.
6. Justify the reasons why your listeners should take advantage of the new idea.
7. Give full details in explaining what course of action should be taken—as soon as possible.

Arrange Your Ideas Into a Speech

Again, study your list of ideas. Choose the ones you want to include in each step of the outline you select—Steps 1, 2, 3, 4, or more—depending on the number of steps you want to use. Within each step, arrange your ideas in any of these adaptable sequences or progressions:

a) From the least interesting to the most interesting;
b) From the least expensive to the most expensive;
c) From the simplest to the most complex;
d) From the ancient or most primitive to the latest and most modern;
e) From the least important to the most important;
f) From the smallest or least significant to the largest and most significant.

In other words, you start with ideas of lesser value and build up to a climax. You give your talk an impact that makes it easy for your listeners to understand and remember your ideas.

Note: You may want to start your talk with an attention-getting idea, and follow it with ideas of lesser importance. If you do, avoid an anticlimax when you're through talking. Reserve some of your most arresting ideas for the conclusion of your talk.

Organize Your Ideas Into Three Basic Parts

Every speech has an opening, a middle, and a closing—so your outline will have three main divisions. With the opening or introduction you should get your listeners' attention, create a favorable atmosphere for what you have to say, stimulate interest in the subject, and clarify what you're going to talk about.

What to Do:

1. To get attention at the start, try one or more of these devices:
   a) Ask a thought-provoking rhetorical question. *Example*: "Ladies and gentlemen: Why is it that every one of us wants prosperity in our town, but hardly anyone wants a prosperous industry to settle here?" You don't really expect your listeners to answer. At this point, you want to open their minds to your point of view. You want their undivided attention.
   b) Make an unusual statement.
   c) Give an offbeat illustration.
   d) Use an effective quotation. But make sure it's concise, directly relevant to the purpose of your talk. *Example*: "I have a young friend who is quite short. Yet he's the star on his school's basketball team. Last night after an exciting game, I asked him, 'Bobby, don't you feel rather small among all those big fellows?' My question did not faze him at all. 'Yes, I do,' he said, 'but I feel like a dime among pennies.' This is exactly the point I want to make tonight, ladies and gentlemen. Compared to our neighbors, our town is small. But we can make it a dime among pennies. All we have to do is to persuade new industries to settle here."
   e) Refer to the current or special interests of your listeners.
   f) Compliment the group, if compliments are applicable.

2. Don't forget to state the purpose or theme of your talk in the introduction, so your listeners will have no doubt why they're there.

Following the introduction, of course, is the outline for the middle or *discussion* of your talk. With the use of main headings and subheadings, fill in all the vital points you want to make. Your outline will help remind you not to stray too far from the subject; not to get wrapped up in so many subordinate points that the main one is lost. *What to Do:*

1. Say clearly what you want the audience to know, to feel, to do.
2. Show why it's important to them to do so.
3. Use the subordinate points to support your central idea, and strengthen your stand with explanation, reasoning, evidence.
4. Define any terms that may not be clear.
5. Repeat ideas to make them stick.
6. Relate each idea to the others for clarity.
7. Include an occasional quote or anecdote to illustrate the points you make.
8. Use examples to show how your main idea works, where it works, when it works, for whom it has already worked. ("This idea was first used five months ago and has since worked very well . . ." "Then Standard Company used it, and they found it worked every time they used it . . ." "And it's particularly effective when used as . . .")

The final step in your outline is the closing or *conclusion*, in which you round out the central idea, summarize and, if necessary, ask for action. The conclusion is not the final stage of the discussion—it's the final section of your talk. It's meant to bring home the whole purpose of your talk.
What to Do:

1. Summarize the main points of your talk.
2. Whenever you can, use an apt quotation.
3. Add urgency to the action you want.
4. Tell a good story. One that knits the purpose of your talk to the speech itself.
5. Repeat your main idea. Briefly, convincingly. *Note*: Many speakers begin the close of a speech with such words as "Now I say . . ." or "So be sure to . . ."
6. Make sure you don't bring in anything new—just reinforce what's already been presented and make clearer the argument you've advanced.
7. Be brief, but don't just stop as if that's all."

There's an old public speaking maxim that's good to keep in mind when preparing your outline. It goes like this: "Tell them what you're going to tell them, tell them, then tell them what you've told them." It's as simple as that!

Points to Remember

—You can either write out your speech, word for word, or develop it mentally. Whichever method you prefer, try to get smooth transition from one idea to the next.

—Use transitional words or phrases to link two different or related ideas, to connect and combine parts of your talk into a smoothly flowing speech.
  Examples:
  "Even so . . ."
  "Therefore . . ."
  "Consequently . . ."
  "Despite this fact . . ."
  "In the first place . . ."
  "For the same reason that . . ."
  "To make clear what I mean . . ."
  "For instance, here's a case that . . ."
  "Now, let's direct our attention to another problem . . ."
  "So, here's what we can do and should do. Right away . . ."

—Practice your speech in front of a mirror. Speak and act naturally. What you do when gesturing during conversation applies to the platform. Gestures lend emphasis to what you say.

—Study your gestures as you rehearse. Be sure to suit your gesture to the word. If your talk calls for rapid speaking, your gestures should be quick. Let them express power, wide sweep, if you use strong volume. If you want to stress a particular point, make your gestures deliberate. *Caution*: Change your pace. Don't go overboard with your gestures.

*Just what qualities constitute a good voice? A good voice is flex-
ible, easily understood, pleasing in quality, and free of affecta-
tions. Of course, an adequate voice doesn't guarantee effective
communication, but it does help a good speech accomplish its
purpose. It serves as a means to an end—the communication of
ideas, information, emotions. A good voice helps you get and
hold the attention of your listeners, command their respect, get
their understanding, and gain their acceptance of your ideas.*

MAKE THE MOST OF YOUR VOICE

Your voice is as distinctively *you* as your thumbprint. It's determined
partly by physical factors—the health and size of your vocal organs,
the length of your vocal cords, your general health. Your personal
traits count, too—your voice gives strong indications of your personality and emotions. Look around you. Chances are you'll find that
the man with the weak and breathy voice isn't a forceful person, and
that the one whose voice can be heard across the room is an extrovert.

So, because your voice is a reflection of your general temperament,
you can't expect radical changes to come quickly. But you can work
on improving your voice until good voice becomes a natural part of
you.

Building a Good Voice

Put all the pieces of your vocal equipment to their best use. That's the
fastest way to change your voice and that's what any good actor
whose voice you admire has done. You have all the equipment he has
—larynx, lungs, throat, mouth, nose, tongue and teeth. Each has its
role in the production of the spoken word. Here are the steps you
can take to improve each stage of your voice production.

Breathing
You have to produce a powerful column of air to set your vocal cords
in action. For that you need adequate lung capacity. Poor posture—
either slouching or stiffness—is the villain that limits your lung capacity. It doesn't help much to correct your posture only when you
stand before an audience. So make it a habit to stand and sit straight
at all times.

Note: Stand erect, your chest lifted, your arms at your sides. Inhale slowly, while raising your arms to shoulder level (don't raise your shoulders). Blow yourself up like a balloon; take air in through you nose and mouth until you feel well expanded, but not strained. Then exhale slowly—with a drawn-out sigh. Repeat, substituting some familiar phrase ("Now is the time for all good men to come to the aid of their party.") for the sigh. Your throat should be relaxed—it's not supposed to get into the act at all. The force should come from deep inside your body. The object is to produce a voice stream which flows easily and continuously. Spend five minutes each morning at this exercise.

Phonation

The second step in tone production is the vibration of the vocal folds in your larynx. Here again, your purpose is defeated if your throat, neck and jaw muscles are tight. Any constriction will limit the fullness of your voice vibrations.

Here's How: Practice singing! There's no better way to achieve muscular freedom, even if you can't carry a tune. A round of ballads each morning as you shower will work wonders.

Resonance

The vibrations from phonation are feeble. So you have to reinforce them. That's the job of your resonators. These include the back of the throat, the nasal cavities in back of the nose, and the head and mouth cavities. Any interference in these sound passages causes nasality—a heavy, thick, clouded tone of voice. So be sure you don't limit their functions.

Here's How: Without letting the muscles of your throat or jaw become tense, practice syllables or words ending in "ng" (*sing, thing, ring, wing*) until you can feel the vibration in back of your nose. Try the same thing with "n" and "m" sounds (*nine, name, send, come, more, thumb*). Read your newspaper aloud; you should hear these nasal consonants as clearly and distinctly as you hear the vowels.

Articulation

This means shaping the resonated tone into sounds, and joining the sounds together into words and phrases. Keep your lips, jaws and tongue nimble so you can adjust them quickly to form different sounds.

Note: Tongue twisters are the most effective aids to articulation. Try these, making sure that every consonant is distinct.

Start slowly. As your articulators become limber, you'll be able to reel them off lickety-split.

(t) The knitted mittens fitted the cute kittens.

(d) Ada needed the seeds for the middle meadow.

(p) Pretty Polly, Patty's pal, typed a heap of papers.

(b) The babe in her blue robe bumped the tub with a cube.

(f) The thief frightened the calf so it fell half down the bluff.

(v) It behooves you to receive the knives he gave as a favor.

(k) Mike the Greek baked a cake in his leaky shack.

(g) The dog tagged after the bugler, wagging his tail and dragging a wig.

(s) Tess missed the geese and the rooster.

(z) Lizzie chose a rose and raspberry pies for the cause.

(sh) Plush cushions with short sashes were the fashion.

(zh) On that occasion the allusion to his decision caused derision.

(ch) The coachman reached the church and searched for his satchel.

(j) Georgeanne kept a budget in the large ledger.

(sts) The pest's nests on the masts and posts were destroyed by the gusts.

(l) Little Lilly fell pell-mell down the hill.

(thd) He writhed about, breathed heavily, and mouthed his words.

(pt) The apt student mapped out a plan, typed quickly, then slept.

(wh) Where and why were you whispering and whimpering?

(w) The women wept over the war waifs and widows.

Listening

An important part of voice building is ear training. Learn to hear your own voice, then you can analyze, evaluate and improve it. Almost all of us are born with pleasant voices. They're impaired by habits we pick up—usually from imitation. When we imitate, we're not being natural. If you have access to a tape recorder, put your voice on tape. The results may startle you—and they may prod you into improving your voice.

Using Your Voice

You've probably been bored silly by people who drone on and on without changing the rate, pitch or force of their voices. Don't let your voice get into that rut! There are a number of ways to get variety into your voice.

Quality

There's no trick for putting quality in your voice. It comes automatically. The more you respond to life around you, the more color you'll get in your voice. If you're a pleasant, sympathetic person, the world will know it from the way you sound. So put a smile in your voice. But it has to be a real one. A forced smile won't fool anyone.

Speaking Rate

Your public speaking rate should average 120 to 150 words a minute. Variations in speed reflect the relative value of what you're saying. Important things are said more slowly than unimportant ones. Learn to pause, without filling the time with those deadly transitions "uh," "um," and "er." Pauses will help you control your speed; they'll give you a chance to emphasize a point and to think ahead to your next thought. Remember, people may be able to hear what you say, but their attention will wander unless you show them what's important by varying your speed.

Pitch

Your normal pitch is the key your voice hits on the musical scale. If you talk at that level all the time, though, the result will be monotonous. Vary your pitch in keeping with the emotional content of what you're saying. A rising inflection denotes doubt or incompleteness of thought; a falling inflection denotes finality. Say the word "yes" at several levels and you'll see how quickly the meaning changes. Just being conscious of your voice level will help you modulate it.

Force

The emphasis you put on words can quickly change the meaning of what you say. For instance, the sentence "I am driving to town" can have five different meanings. It can be a simple informative statement, it can tell *who* is driving, it can be defiant, it can show the method of getting there, or it can indicate that the destination is one place rather than another. Put the emphasis where it belongs to convey the message you want to get across.

The English language offers us some half million words. Yet the average American uses only 3,000 of them! You can't buy, borrow or steal language. The only way to get it is by using it. And this means simply that you must get the "word habit." Of course, you shouldn't choose your words just to show off your vocabulary. But you should have command of enough words to communicate clearly and precisely. Your words should be appropriate for you, your audience and the situation. High-flown or technical words and stilted phrases aren't your own—it isn't YOU speaking when you use them. They may differ so much from your ordinary speech that your listeners will know they're borrowed.

ADD COLOR AND IMPACT TO YOUR SPEECH

Your ideas are more apt to be accepted if you use clear, understandable, vivid language—words that have punch and drive, and words that have color and picture quality.

The best words are simple words which give vivid mental images. You have hundreds of these words in your vocabulary but you probably never use them in speaking. Why? Because you have three vocabularies—for reading, for writing, and for speaking. Your speaking vocabulary is the smallest of all. You can improve your speaking vastly by using many of the lively words from your other two vocabularies.

Visualize Your Ideas
When you're talking, you're not thinking words. You're thinking mental pictures, ideas which you hope to convey to your audience. In order to communicate your ideas, you have to use the words that fit them. If you use strong, clear and distinct words, your listeners will get forceful, understandable mental pictures. You already have these words—so pluck them out, dust them off and put them to use.

Picture Your Ideas
Use words that stir your listeners' imagination—words that paint images for them. If your listeners "see," they'll understand. One way to stimulate images is to express your ideas in the language of the senses—sight, hearing, smell, touch, taste.

What to Do:

1. Use words that give visual impressions: jaundiced, snub-nosed, knock-kneed, red-eyed, freckle-faced, flashing, glowing, grimy, sparkling.
2. Use words that suggest movement: slide, dash, steal, vault, plunge, surge.
3. Use words that suggest sounds: splash, clatter, crash, splutter, drone.
4. Use words that suggest sense of touch: cold, icy, hot, smooth, greasy, slippery, slimy, rough.

Here are some brain-teasers to put you in practice. Write down your answers and see how many words you can bring forward from the back of your mind.

a. Almost every word has a synonym—a word which could substitute for it. Some have hundreds! See how many synonyms you can find for these words: bright, expert, bad, bare, confuse, elevate, fury, holy, innocent, move, prove, short, young, said, walk.
b. Antonyms are words with the opposite meanings. Think of as many antonyms as you can for each of these words: beautiful, calm, dim, fame, good, large, misfortune, proud, rich, sad.
c. These words all have several meanings. See how many you know: strike, brief, spade, bite, crown, detect, drive, enter, find, grate, hang, job, kill, mate, pattern.
d. There are many words which are general—and colorless. See how many specific, colorful words you can substitute for each of these: act, animal, capture, cry, event, mad, person, run, show, top.
e. Find words to replace these trite, overused words: great, lovely, adorable, darling, exceedingly, gorgeous, marvelous, most, nice, precious, really, stupid, tremendous, very.

Idioms

Idioms are groups of words with vivid connotations, pithy expressions that suggest striking and sensuous impressions. They'll give your speech a lift if you'll use them occasionally—but use them only when you can do it comfortably. Figurative language should never be contrived.

Note: Look at these familiar idioms— notice how the mental pictures come right at you.

hold on	in a stew	take it off your
take a break	bar the door	hands
hot and bothered	simmer down	give the green light
settle down	stop in your tracks	sound off
get a move on	lap it up	raring to go
head in the	up in the air	feet on the ground
clouds	wash one's hands of	

Personal Language
Use personal pronouns. You'll involve your audience if you spatter your talk with *I, we, you, ours.* And, in oral language, contractions are perfectly acceptable. *You'll* is better than *you will; they've* is more natural than *they have.*

Action Words
The active voice is more forceful than the passive. So use it! Why say, "For it is well do it," when "Do it" is so much clearer? Or "For it is believed . . ." when "We know . . ." does the trick? Keep your language moving. Another way to achieve action is to cut adverbs and adjectives to a minimum. They slow you down and keep you from getting to the point of your talk. And, in most instances, you don't even need them.

Words to Avoid
Your words should *not* be noticed by your listeners. They're just the bricks your statements are built from. But they will be noticed if they're the wrong words—if they're inappropriate, or if they don't blend with the general character of your speech. Here are the categories of words which should not be used. Weed them out of your speech.

Vulgarisms
Acceptable words are those that meet the standards observed by educated people in careful conversation. Words that fall below these standards won't endear you to your listeners—not even in private conversation. And in public speaking they're absolutely taboo. So beware of off-color words and such grammatical earsores as "ain't" and "hadn't ought to."

Slang
Don't use slang if you can think of another way to express your idea.

In most instances, you'll find there are good English expressions that are just as vigorous. Avoid all slang in formal situations.

Pedagoguese

Steer clear of long words and high-sounding phrases. They're a sign of ignorance. Instead, aim for a thorough knowledge of simple words. Economize!

What to Do: These are examples of typical "pedagoguese," and simpler substitutes.

Stilted	*Natural*
commence	begin
endeavor	try
consume	eat
contemplate	think
myself	me
utilize	use
conflagration	fire
due to the fact that	because
succeeds in achieving	gets
took the opportunity of saying	said

Clichés

Clichés are familiar phrases which have become hackneyed. They make your ideas sound hackneyed, too. Establish yourself as an original thinker.

What to Do: Avoid such phrases as—

too funny for words	no sooner said than done
last but not least	method in his madness
at a loss for words	hard as a rock
it stands to reason	black as pitch
goes without saying	what in the world
gives me great pleasure	as I was saying

Euphemisms

Euphemisms are mild or indirect words that we substitute for offensive ones. Unfortunately, though, they can be irritating—especially if the original words really aren't offensive. It's better to use "die" than "pass away," "leg" than "limb," "eat" than "partake."

Technical and Foreign Words

Some technical words may be necessary. But if your audience isn't thoroughly familiar with them, explain them fully. Foreign words, on the other hand, are seldom necessary. For one thing, they're pretentious. For another, your audience may not get the message. Of course, a large number of foreign words are now part of our language. These naturalized words are fine—because they're almost universally understood.

Use the Precise Word

Although your speaking vocabulary should be simple, it doesn't have to be limited. Vivid speech is precise speech. You can't be precise unless the right words are at your command. So build your vocabulary. Get yourself some brand-new words. Learn them, use them, and become comfortable with them. You'll find they'll pop out when you need them because they're part of you.

What to Do:

1. Read! Include good books as well as newspapers and magazines. Jot down new words in a notebook.
2. Refer! Use the dictionary as soon as you find a new word. Be sure its meaning or meanings are clear. Then refer to your notebook often.
3. Write! One of the best ways to use your new words is to spend a few minutes each day writing a paragraph or two—your observations, your feelings about the weather, your job—any topic. With a little effort you can work your new words in. Then they won't be so strange when it's time to use them in speaking.
4. Listen! Some of the most stimulating language you'll hear is available at the flick of your television or FM radio dial. Listen to some good talk when you're driving, working around the house, relaxing. And listen to your co-workers and your friends. Soon you'll notice the good, expressive words they use effectively—also the ones that bother you, the ones you'll want to avoid.
5. Speak! When you do have command of your new words, don't hesitate to use them. Just remember, they're not really part of you until you can use them without calling attention to yourself.

Words act as signals. It stands to reason that these signals must be clear and familiar to your audience. For words to be clear they must be enunciated *distinctly. Enunciation is a matter of articulating precisely the sounds you should be producing. If you've ever had to take mumbled directions with dropped syllables and clipped or run-together words, you're well acquainted with faulty enunciation and the problems it creates.*

MAKE YOURSELF UNDERSTOOD

For words to be familiar they must be *pronounced* as the audience is used to hearing them. Pronunciation involves choosing the correct sound and placing the proper stress on the accented syllable or syllables. Proper pronunciation requires awareness of the way words are said in your locality.

People are quick to notice variations from their pronunciation habits. Yet there's no positive law—no court to say what's right and what isn't—not even the dictionary. Pronunciation is established by custom. Violate the custom and you'll interfere with the audience's concentration on your message. And you could cause plenty of resentment.

But this doesn't mean you should change a New England way of speaking when you're visiting in the Deep South. In fact, you'd sound phony affecting a Southern accent. On the other hand, many words— and particularly proper names—do have more than one correct pronunciation. And, when you can make a choice without a show of affectation, you should favor the pronunciation of the locality.

The United States has varying customs according to locality, rather than one standard American pronunciation. The three main standards (or customs), based on the geographical regions where they're used, are Eastern (New England and New York), Southern (states of the Old South), and General American (spoken elsewhere). These sectional peculiarities, as a rule, don't interfere with the comprehension of speech. Your way of talking won't be objectionable unless your accent is extreme or your pronunciation is incorrect by *every* U.S. standard.

Since approximately two thirds of the people in the country use General American speech, the national radio and television systems use this dialect. Dictionaries, also, use General American pronunciation because their job is to record the pronunciation currently in use by the majority of the educated population. If usage justifies, they record a second pronunciation.

Your pronunciation, generally, should be the accepted pronunciation of your locality. It is the "best" pronunciation for you because it will pass unnoticed in any cultured group.

Words to Watch—Enunciation

Some of our most familiar words are treated the most shabbily—by slurring or skipping vowels or consonants. Enunciate them clearly.

What to Do:

1. Enunciate even the little words—they're important. Don't say:

uv	for of	kin	for can
frum	for from	ketch	for catch
wuz	for was	un	for and
fer	for for	nd	for and
thum	for them	becuz	for because

2. Take a little longer to pronounce the *whole* word, so you won't omit a sound or syllable. Avoid saying:

ac'rate	for accurate	hist'ry	for history
an'ar'tic	for antarctic	lib'ary	for library
b'come	for become	liter'ture	for literature
b'lieve	for believe	mir'r	for mirror
can'idate	for candidate	p'lice	for police
cap'tal	for capital	p'lite	for polite
choc'late	for chocolate	pop'lar	for popular
circ'lar	for circular	pos'tively	for positively
comp'ny	for company	re'ly	for really
di'mond	for diamond	reco'nize	for recognize
dif'rent	for different	reg'lar	for regular
exper'ment	for experiment	soph'more	for sophomore
gener'ly	for generally	s'pose	for suppose
gov'nor	for governor	ter'r	for terror
g'ography	for geography	usu'ly	for usually

These two common Latin words need all their sounds, too:
bona fide is said "bona fide" ("fide" to rhyme with "side")
vice versa is said "vice-a versa"

Words to Watch—Pronunciation

There are hundreds of words which are widely mispronounced—some because of misplaced syllable accent, some because of reversal of sounds, some because they're pronounced the way they're spelled, some because a syllable or sound is added, some because they're associated with a similar word which is pronounced differently. Learn to say them correctly.

What to Do:
1. These are words often mispronounced because of improperly placed accent. The capitalized syllable is the one which should receive the stress:

aCUmen	FORmidable	PRECedence
adDRESS	freQUENTer	PRECedent (noun)
ADmirable	GENuine	preCEDent (adj.)
ADulatory	GONdola	PREFerable
ADversary	GRIMace	preTENSE
alLY	HOSpitable	PREValent
aWRY	IMpotent	pyRAMidal
bapTIZE	inCOGnito	reCOIL
beNEFicent	inEXplicable	reMEdiable
braVAdo	INfamous	REPutable
BRIGand	INfluence	RESpite
CERebral	irREVocable	roBUST
clanDEStine	JOCund	rouTINE
COMparable	LAMentable	seCREtive
conDOLence	maNIacal	suPERfluous
DESpicable	misANthropy	syRINGE
DIRigible	MISchievous	tarPAUlin
eLECtoral	MObile	THEatre
exCESS	pleBEian	traVAIL
EXigency	poLICE	VAgary
EXquisite	POSThumous	VEhement

If some of these words aren't in your vocabulary, it's a good list to start your vocabulary cultivation program. Look them up—and use them!

2. Watch yourself on these words. They're frequently said incorrectly because sounds within them are reversed. The word in parentheses is the wrong way:

cavalry	(calvary)	modern	(modren)
children	(childern)	perspiration	(prespiration)
hundred	(hunderd)	pharynx	(pharnyx)
larynx	(larnyx)	prescription	(perscription)

3. Since our English alphabet isn't consistently phonetic—representative of the same sounds—you can't always pronounce a word the way it's spelled. When saying the following words, *avoid* pronouncing the sounds in parentheses:

a(l)mond	fore(h)ead
apropo(s)	parl(i)ament
bla(ck)guard	picayun(e)
bus(i)ness	epis(t)le
ca(l)m	sa(l)mon
coyot(e)	vi(c)t(u)als
extr(a)ordinary	Wo(rce)ste(r)shire

Also be aware of the correct pronunciation of these words:

bade	is said	bad
chameleon	is said	kameleon
chic	is said	sheek or shick
flaccid	is said	flaksid
hiccough	is said	hiccup
machination	is said	makination
quay	is said	key
err	rhymes with	fur
fungi	rhymes with	sponge-eye

4. Here are several words which are adequate without adding syllables or sounds (shown in parentheses):

ath(a)lete	el(u)m
casual(i)ty	fil(u)m
chim(i)ney	hein(i)ous
cor(o)net	mischiev(i)ous
drown(d)ed	umb(e)rella

5. And finally, some words may come out wrong because they're improperly associated with a word or part of a word which is similar, but pronounced differently. How many times have your heard these said incorrectly—rhyming with, or taking on by mistake, the sounds of the words in parentheses?

column	(volume)	hearth	(earth)
comely	(homely)	height	(length)
despicable	(despise)	impious	(pious)
February	(January)	maintenance	(maintain)
granary	(grain)	penalize	(penalty)
grievous	(previous)	pronunciation	(pronounce)

Effective delivery requires coordination of your mind, voice, language and body. Besides auditory signs or signals (words), it uses visual signs (body movement, facial expression, posture, gestures). Your delivery, like your speech itself, should be appropriate to the total speaking situation. Properly done, it's simple, unaffected, direct, communicative and conversational. There's no need to be "on stage"—you're a speaker, not an exhibitionist. A good delivery will enable you to establish rapport with your audience and to use up nervous energy—put your tensions to constructive use.

MAKE YOUR TALK VISUALLY EFFECTIVE

The speaker with good delivery is enthusiastic, and he shows it. A detached attitude is fatal, and you can't be enthusiastic unless you believe in what you're going to say. Imagination is the basis for enthusiasm—so cultivate it.

Remember to talk to your listeners not just to yourself. And adapt your delivery to the kind of message you have to convey, as well as to the situation. Good platform delivery is an extension of good conversation; it has the same intimacy and awareness of the reactions of others. In any speaking situation, your goal is to be poised and at ease, modest and unassuming, with a natural sincerity and self-confidence. Above all, your friendliness must be genuine. If it's simulated, your audience will know it.

Bodily Action

Silent expression—the excessive power of your looks, posture and movement—is just as important as your oral expression. Your body action and your language must be harmonious.

Meaningful body action comes spontaneously from your inner feelings. It includes movements of your whole body, movements of parts of your body (gestures), facial expressions and posture. In normal conversation, you speak naturally with gestures and with your whole body. It's only when conversation takes place in an out-of-the-ordinary situation—as in public speaking—that you become inhibited. Your body actions can feel and appear unnatural. And, if they're weak, indefinite, poorly timed or belabored, your listeners are sure to notice.

Effective body action can clarify your ideas and express your emotions—reinforce what you have to say. But body movements should be purposeful and sparingly used.

It's not only the overt movements of your head, arms, shoulders and whole body that can affect the impression the audience has of you. Those slightly discernible movements of the muscles of your arms, shoulders or face may give an audience accurate indications of your feelings and attitudes. From these involuntary actions listeners form opinions of your responsiveness, sincerity, decisiveness, sympathy and confidence.

Posture

Bearing and posture indicate health, vigor, alertness. They can also indicate characteristics of superiority or inferiority. Superiority is the attitude that any audience resents most. And inferiority on the platform is disastrous—the audience won't respect you. Make sure your appearance doesn't indicate weakness; a sagging, listless manner, and negative bearing will do it. Straighten up! Stand in a position that's easy—one that leaves you free to move and express yourself, yet still invites confidence. Stand still. Don't pace, shift your weight, sway, rock or bounce. Avoid random movements. Variety in posture is desirable, but changes should come normally during transitions in your talk. If you're sure of yourself and make every effort to stay in control, you'll look the part of the speaker.

Facial Expressions

Let your face be as expressive in talking to a group as it is in conversation. Let your feelings show. Remember your eyes are the most expressive feature of your face—look at your audience. Move your gaze. Let your face show that you're reacting to them, conversing *with* and not just talking *at* them. If you spread your eye contact around, your eyes will be able to help the straight flow of ideas from you to your listeners. Looking over their heads doesn't fool anybody.

Gestures

Normally, gestures are natural and spontaneous. No one keeps his body and arms absolutely still. Good gestures require coordinated use of the whole body and should be properly timed, definite and freely made. They should vary in vigor with the ideas expressed. They should be appropriate. Try to avoid erratic, unnecessary gestures. Bold, free movements are best. But if they're planned, they may appear awkward. Then they'll no longer support your speech—they'll detract from it. That most subtle enemy of the speaker—monotony—

applies to gesture and movement, too. Change of position affords relief, but remember that it should be relevant to your words. The use of your hands figures in. Talk with them—use them to *show* your ideas.

Here's How:
1. Make most of your gestures above the waist—gestures made below the waist indicate failure, defeat, despair. Try it in front of a mirror, and you'll see the difference immediately.
2. If you're using your hands to hold outline cards, keep your forearms roughly parallel with your waist, with your elbows out about three inches from the sides. Elbows held too closely are awkward and tend to weaken your authority.
3. Place your hands lightly on the lectern if you have one, but don't lean on it.
4. Don't let your hands flap around. Lax hands indicate a lack of power and leadership.
5. Use *both* hands to be a fully operating speaker.

Mannerisms
Behavior employed so frequently that it calls attention to itself is called a mannerism. Dozens of these distracting behavior patterns are used by public speakers—to the detriment of their delivery and, therefore, their communication. Mannerisms are acquired as releases for nervous energy, substitutes for pauses, test periods for thinking what to say next. They may be unconscious and can become habitual. Guard against allowing them to slip into your delivery.

Note: Avoid these 10 common mannerisms—
1. Fiddling with a pencil, or eyeglasses.
2. Adjusting clothes and picking lint off them.
3. Winding your watch.
4. Drumming fingers on the table.
5. Misusing the lectern by grasping or leaning on it.
6. Slumping posture.
7. Studying everything but the audience—lack of direct eye contact.
8. Excessive bodily action.
9. Wandering around the platform.
10. Making extraneous sounds and vocalizing pauses (ah, uh, er).

How to Overcome Fear

There are few people who don't know the panicky feeling of stage fright—racing heart, dry lips and mouth, butterflies. Stage fright is probably the primary reason people shrink from getting up to talk.

First step in overcoming it is realizing that *all* speakers get butterflies. Any time we step out of our mold of ordinary group conversation (where there's equal responsibility on each of the speakers), tensions are bound to mount. Suddenly the focus is on us. We have to "go it alone," bear full responsibility for the formal presentation of ideas in front of an audience. Fortunately, the tensions are more apparent to the speaker than to the audience.

Frustrating as the prospect of stage fright is, its tension can contribute to your success as a speaker. Anxiety increases your desire to do well, prods you to prepare, makes you alert and energetic while speaking. It speeds up your thinking processes and causes you to become sensitive to audience reactions. In other words, you profit from turning your nervousness into dynamic energy.

However, the feeling of responsibility is the *only* commendable cause for nervousness. If your anxiety stems from a feeling of inferiority, perhaps you need to straighten out your sense of values. Talk it over with an experienced friend. The third cause of nervousness—and the most common—is lack of preparation, the result of sheer laziness. You shouldn't attempt to leave the mold of normal group conversation unless you're willing to spend the time necessary to develop yourself and your subject.

What to Do: The secrets of reducing stage fright are essentially those of getting your mind off yourself and directing your energies to more profitable diversions. Here are a half dozen—

1. Prepare and plan. There's no substitute. The perfect requisites for confidence are a well-organized speech and an interesting subject.
2. Practice. Remember, nothing will help you as much in public speaking as private practicing. You'll find it helps to decrease your feelings of anxiety. Talk through your speech to an imaginary audience, or ask someone in your family to listen. If you have an opportunity to take a course in speech, you'll find the training will help promote confidence in general, as well as in the formal speaking situation.
3. Relax. Here's the reason for using your whole body to speak. Nervousness and muscle tension work in a vicious circle. You

may have to practice the art of relaxation as you practice your delivery. In order to keep your breathing as nearly normal as possible, try inhaling slowly to a count as you sit waiting to give your talk.

4. Adopt a positive attitude. Audiences come to hear, not to condemn. Give yourself a mental pep talk. Remember you earned the right to speak—otherwise you wouldn't have been asked. So speak up to the audience, make them know you expect to succeed. Speak out with authority.

5. Get speaking experience. It's the best teacher. Volunteer to talk before a group, no matter how small, whenever you have the opportunity. You'll begin to get the hang of it, and know what to expect when the important moment arrives.

6. Force your audience to "converse" with you. They're not supposed to talk back, but their expression will enable you to respond to them and to gauge your effectiveness. Often you can bring them into the speech situation. On some occasions the introduction of a question-and-answer period will help.

Act Like a Professional Speaker

Follow the customs of courtesy applicable in any social situation. First, dress appropriately for the occasion. Your appearance is the thing on which you're first judged. If your clothing is ludicrous for the event—no matter how appropriate for another situation—you'll be remembered as "that man in the silly suit."

Second, be punctual. You'll lose respect if you run in late, no matter the excuse. Be pleasant and businesslike—a speech is not a social occasion.

When the time comes, walk confidently to the front of the group. Be relaxed. If you're called on to speak and have been sitting on a platform in front of the audience, take care to rise gracefully. In order to rise and to sit without doubling up, learn to balance yourself by supporting the weight of your body on one leg and foot, letting the other foot slip in and out from under the chair.

All eyes will be on you as you come before your audience. So remember the list of taboo mannerisms. Don't adjust your tie or jingle your key chain. Stand away from the edge of the platform, and don't lean on the table. If you bring an outline with you, lay it inconspicuously on the speaker's stand or keep it at your side until you've established contact with your audience.

Importance of Beginning Your Talk

Your first job is to recognize the group before you. Pause before talking—look at your audience. Some occasions may permit "Mr. Chairman, Ladies and Gentlemen," but not *all* occasions. If you do use these salutations, use them in an intimate, friendly manner, as if you were actually addressing individually each member of the audience. On most occasions, a genuine smile and a nod to your introducer—don't ignore him—are enough. Manner and attitude can be a greeting in themselves. But either way, verbally or silently, you should greet those you're going to address. Standing and waiting for them to be quiet may in itself be a salutation.

If your audience is large or you're speaking outdoors, you may have to speak more slowly and a little louder at the start in order to get attention. But don't fade out later. During your speech, be deliberate—erect, direct, assuring. Extreme haste or delay makes you look apprehensive. Utilize pauses. Have an attitude of friendliness.

And don't forget your audience. Watch for the signs that will tell you you're going too quickly or are right on the beam. Audiences usually are sympathetic. If you allow their attention to lapse, you've had it—you're going it alone.

Limit your talk to the suggested time. You might be asked to answer questions—if you are, don't use the time for extra speech making. Be brief with your answers so there's time for everyone to ask a question. If you don't know an answer, say so.

Importance of Ending Your Talk

When you say "in conclusion," mean it. End your talk forcefully—don't peter out. Your audience wants you to speak well, then sit down.

Conclude your speech graciously by acknowledging the audience. Without this transition between speech and no speech, there's apt to be a shock—the finishing will seem too abrupt. Better speakers avoid "I thank you"; it's used too often and it suggests perfunctory humility. The most acceptable way of making the transition is by a pause and attitude appropriate to the conclusion—frequently a friendly nod and smile are all you need. Finish with dignity. Pause, then walk away firmly, erect.

SUBJECT INDEX

C

Cab Drivers, see also 10.65, 40.21, 156.54, 592.64, 762.49

Caddy, see also 718.26, 718.29, 718.49, 718.76

California, see also 156.56

Camels, see also 60.49

Campaign, see also 140.46, 454.54, 592.37, 592.54, 592.57

Camping/Camp, see also 152.58, 152.62, 202.53

Canasta, see also 328.24

Cancellation, see also 762.38

Candidate, see also 156.53, 592.48

Candy, see also 40.63, 110.55

Cannibals/Cannibalism, see also 40.72, 312.22, 312.27, 312.38, 592.53

Capitalism, see also 592.56

Capitol Hill, 592.44

Capone, Al, 208.62

Cards, see also 328.24, 328.34, 328.41, 328.43, 338.53

Career, see also 302.33, 430.39

Carefulness (see also Caution), see also 524.48

Caribbean, 712.41

Cars/Driving, see also 10.51, 10.-57, 10.58, 10.62, 10.66, 30.47, 60.51, 96.57, 152.62, 156.64, 240.54, 328.37, 338.52, 338.57, 416.50, 430.33, 430.35, 480.43, 484.51, 602.56, 666.50, 666.51, 666.52, 718.22, 718.71, 756.47, 798.53, 814.40, 824.55

Carnivals, see also 328.30

Casket, see also 302.06

Casualties, see also 718.73

Cats, see also 60.45, 500.58

Cause, see also 592.34

Caution (see also Carefulness), see also 60.33, 402.55

Celebrations, see also 10.59, 20.54, 40.69, 328.45, 514.54

Celebrities, see also 302.07, 680.50, 750.51, 762.51, 806.45, 814.48, 814.50

Cellar, see also 386.52

Cemetery, see also 338.51

Census, see also 302.69

Chair, see also 302.47

Chairman, see also 232.33

Champion, see also 770.50

Chance (see also Luck), see also 110.65, 328.25, 718.58

Change, see also 110.52, 168.70, 170.53, 592.63, 612.50, 788.53, 804.51

Character(s), see also 120.54, 592.59

Charge Account (see also Credit), see also 494.43

Charity, see also 96.60, 152.45, 294.43, 302.09

Charm, see also 814.56

Chase, see also 10.60, 30.42, 718.-74

Chastity, see also 534.56

Chauffeurs, see also 430.33, 602.-56, 798.51

Cheating, see also 718.36, 718.54

Checkers, see also 328.29

Checks, see also 202.61, 302.11, 302.21, 302.29, 302.83

Cheerfulness, see also 22.58

Chess, see also 120.51

Chicken, see also 60.37, 60.55, 60.57

Child/Children, see also 20.51, 30.44, 40.41, 40.67, 60.46, 60.62, 156.50, 156.52, 156.54, 180.56, 208.59, 294.40, 294.45, 430.35, 442.55, 500.58, 502.56, 656.24, 656.31, 672.42, 672.45, 742.41, 824.54

Childhood (see also Children), see also 30.66, 156.63

China/Chinese, see also 554.53, 592.49

Choice, see also 294.38, 328.28, 672.78, 804.59

Chorus Girl, see also 266.45

Christmas, see also 338.53, 378.51

Church (see also Religion), see also 20.56, 156.50, 302.06, 302.51, 302.70, 328.36, 494.90, 514.52, 546.52, 622.51, 656.20, 672.35, 718.72

Circumstances, see also 602.57

Circus, see also 60.35, 266.44, 266.46, 524.50

Cities (see also New York, Los Angeles, etc.), see also 22.54, 40.59, 50.50, 140.56, 202.68, 240.54, 240.55, 240.57, 756.47

Civil Rights, see also 96.56

Claims, see also 140.34, 442.52

W

Y

Z